WHOLE LOTTA SHAKIN'

A ROCK & ROLL LOVER'S REFLECTIONS ON LIFE, LIBERTY, AND THE PURSUIT OF HAPPINESS

RODNEY LEE

Ambassador Books, Inc.
Worcester • Massachusetts

Other Works by Rodney Lee

God Is Our Co-Pilot
Shoe Town

Library of Congress Cataloging-in-Publication Data

Lee, Rodney, 1945-
Whole lotta shakin' : a rock & roll lover's reflections on life,
liberty, and the pursuit of happiness / Rodney Lee.
p. cm.
ISBN 978-1-929039-45-6 (pbk.)
1. Rock music--History and criticism. 2. Lee, Rodney, 1945- I. > Title.

ML3534.L423 2007
781.66--dc22
2007027783

Published in the United States by Ambassador Books, Inc.
91 Prescott Street, Worcester, Massachusetts 01605
(800) 577-0909

Printed in the United States.

Cover design by Cheryl Greene, Worcester, Massachusetts
Cover photo by James H. Finnegan, Finnegan Photographers, Worcester, Massachusetts

To Amanda Marie (Lee) Peloquin,
the sweetest soul I know.

ACKNOWLEDGEMENTS

J ust as a bank owes its solvency to its depositors, I am indebted first and foremost to Greg Mangan for the encouragement and support he has offered as *Whole Lotta Shakin'* took shape. Greg's standard question whenever we conversed over lunch and at other times was, "How's the book coming along?" Or, "Is the book done yet?" Greg's persistent prodding and enthusiastic endorsement inspired me to finish the job when the going got rough. To my wife, who read several chapters early on and pronounced them fit for public consumption, I say, "Merci, my sweet Marie!" My gratitude is extended as well to my newspaper colleague Dick Broszeit for his continued championing of my writing endeavors, to my professional associates and fellow Rock & Roll devotees Luisa Heffernan and Jody DiBella for their strong interest in this work, to Vince Hemmeter for permitting us to shoot pictures for the cover of the book "on location" at Ralph's (a storied Worcester, Massachusetts club), to Jim and Pat Finnegan for the diligence, commitment and excellent judgment they demonstrated in the session at Ralph's that brought visuals of the band The Silverbacks front and center, to Greg Munro and Charlene Arsenault for the aid they rendered in my efforts to publicize their '50s cover band Cathy's Clown, to Mike Lynch and Cliff Goodwin of The Silverbacks for agreeing to participate in this project, to my cousin Joyce More for her love, to Cheryl Greene for the creative energy she brought to the design of the jacket of the book and last but certainly not least to local radio deejays Paul Lauzon and Milton Cordeiro. Paul and Milton's Oldies Rock & Roll shows on WCUW in Worcester help keep a precious era in musical history alive—and bring glee to my heart as I listen in each week. I look forward to "Echoes of the Past" and "Doo Wop All Night Long." As The Beatles would say (I'm paraphrasing here), "Roll over, Beethoven, I got a record for my DJ to play!" Or as Paul Lauzon himself would put it, "Let's shake a little tail feather!" Long live Rock & Roll!

TABLE OF CONTENTS

Photo by James H. Finnegan of Finnegan Photographers, Worcester, MA.

Pictured hanging out on stage at Ralph's, a popular club in Worcester, Massachusetts, are The Silverbacks, a local band whose forte is maximum Rhythm & Blues. From left to right are Cliff Goodwin, Laurie Kollios, Mike Lynch, Bill McGillivray and Jim Perry. The same group is shown in a slightly different configuration (with James Dean "looking on") on the front cover.

INTRODUCTION

A perceptive person once said, "Music makes the world go round." As is the case with so many expressions that ring true from the moment they are uttered, the phrase was picked up by the wind and carried to the corners of the globe. It became commonplace. As time passed and music evolved, Rock & Roll pushed its way onto the stage; suddenly, as a result, the earth spun even faster and more intensely on its axis. Adults, hearing the bold new sound and feeling the powerful vibrations for the first time, recoiled in dismay. They buckled in and held on for dear life. Teenagers, however, celebrated; their view was, "let the joy ride proceed!" Drums thundered; guitars wailed; singers shouted and stomped. The artists and the bands poured forth from small towns and big cities. They took their acts and their aspirations to smoky clubs and cavernous gymnasiums and giant stadiums and stuffy halls and drafty recording studios. Now, an entire generation looked beyond the quiet calm of the 1950s in its search for love, fun, thrills and fulfillment. Its members finished high school, came of age to drink and vote and went off to college, to serve in Vietnam, to protest the war, to marry and have children, to find careers; and, amid this flurry of activity, to form opinions about Life, Liberty and the Pursuit of Happiness. A "Whole Lotta Shakin' " had begun!

Photo by James H. Finnegan

It is a singular privilege to be the grandparent of seven little darlings (eight, if an honorary add-on is included). All share my love for "the convertible life," which makes "the ride" that much more enjoyable. Pictured with me in the back yard of the home of Photographer Jim Finnegan and his wife Pat are, from the left (all ages applicable as of the summer of '06): Caitlin Noel, 15; Alexis Mary Elizabeth, 11; Jordan Nicole, 12; Kelcie Ann, 6; Emily Grace, 7; David Michael, 8; Amelia Beatrice, 4; and Abagayle Rose, 7. (Kelcie Ann is a member of the family by virtue of the ease with which she assimilated herself into the group).

I. CONVERTIBLES

"Ridin' along in my automobile
My baby beside me at the wheel
I stole a kiss at the turn of a mile
My curiosity running wild…"

"No Particular Place To Go"
Chuck Berry
Chess Records, 1964

C huck Berry and I share the same birthday (October 18th—1926 and 1945, respectively), which makes him nineteen years my senior. It also places him on the front lines of the Rock & Roll revolution, alongside the medium's other early greats. Indeed, just as golf had its "Big Three" (Arnold Palmer, Gary Player and Jack Nicklaus, who, with the help of television, put the game on the map), Rock & Roll has its "Legends:" Chuck Berry, Jerry Lee Lewis and Little Richard, all still, thankfully, alive and performing at this time. Charles Edward Anderson "Chuck" Berry officially broke through at the ripe old age of thirty; initially a devotee of Nat King Cole and Muddy Waters, he first rocked the house at a high school musical show in his native St. Louis with a rendition of a Jay McShann blues song called "Confessin' the Blues." With applause ringing in his ears, he decided then and there that he was born to perform. It wasn't until he met Leonard Chess of Chess Records in Chicago more than a decade later that Chuck Berry attracted notice, however. Chess liked a Bob Wills song Chuck Berry had done called "Ida Red." The rewrite became "Maybellene." Famed D.J. Alan Freed loved

"Maybellene" so much that he played it over and over, and it vaulted into the top five on the record charts. With this success serving as an impetus, more hits followed: "Johnny B. Goode," "Memphis," "Roll Over Beethoven," "Brown Eyed Handsome Man," "School Days." Eventually dubbed "Mr. Rock 'n' Roll," Chuck Berry's acclaim once he'd arrived stretched overseas to the UK; it even survived a twenty-month stay in prison after he was arrested on a morals charge. This incarceration almost cost him his career; a silly tune he recorded in concert in 1972, "Mr. Ding A Ling," which became a fan favorite, and his celebrated "duck walk," helped turn things around. Today, Chuck Berry is justifiably recognized as one of Rock's all-time greats. A charter member of the Rock & Roll Hall of Fame (he was inducted in 1986), he inspired countless fellow artists including: The Rolling Stones, The Beatles, The Beach Boys and Elvis Presley. One of the highest compliments he ever received came from the late John Lennon, who said, "If you tried to give Rock & Roll another name, you might call it 'Chuck Berry.' "

Few "car songs" measure up to Chuck Berry's "No Particular Place To Go" for rollicking good-time Rock & Roll. Members of my generation can identify with "cruisin' and playin' the radio," "cuddlin' more and drivin' slow," stealing a kiss and parking "way out on the Kokomo." Likewise, few indulgences surpass setting out for a drive with the top rolled back and the radio tuned to the "Oldies" station, on a Saturday or Sunday afternoon, with no specific destination in mind and with no urgency to return anytime soon.

Owning a convertible is one of those singular privileges—akin, in my estimation, to holding the deed to a mountainside villa that overlooks the sea.

Of course there is a price, often severe, to be paid, as there is for any luxury item, whether it be a forty-foot sloop, a fourteen-carat diamond ring or a Rolex watch. My own "pound of flesh" is exacted by the holder of the lien every thirty days, and is so excruciatingly painful that it is a wonder the neighbors cannot hear my screams of anguish when the checkbook is broken out at the end of each month.

If the sole determinant in assessing whether the honor is "worth" the expense were the number of days of the year that the top (made of canvas, a formidably resilient and thus tremendously appreciated material) can be lowered under a powdery blue sky, with the temperature soaring toward eighty degrees Fahrenheit, any sane person would have to answer in the negative. This is especially the case for those of us who reside in a maliciously inhospitable northern clime like New England, where convertible (and swimming-pool) weather that could be viewed as unquestionably without flaw comes around about as often as a big hit on the slot machines at Foxwoods or Mohegan Sun.

Then again, few pleasures in life are quite so sublime as driving past a local pond and hearing a boy on a bicycle—his eyes larger than saucers—shout in your ears, "Nice car!" Or tooling along Hull Shore Drive in Nantasket Beach and realizing that leather-clad members of the biker crowd hanging out at the Dry Dock aren't the only people enjoying the sweetness of a soft summer night. Or nodding in a sort of condescending fashion as co-workers—noticing "The Car" leaving the parking lot at five o'clock—flash a thumb's-up, as if to say, "Way to go!" Or having your grandson (David Michael, aka "Mikey")—always extremely inquisitive—ask, just before he is buckled into the back seat, "Pop, can we put the roof down?"

It was my good fortune to be hooked up with a convertible for an all-too-brief period of time upon meeting my future bride; she even had the good sense (or the bad judgment, depending on how you look at it) to let me take her pale-yellow '67 Volkswagen with the black top back to Virginia Beach from Vestal, New York, when I was stationed at Little Creek, Virginia. There is a tendency when such an object is placed in your hands for the thrill to go to your head, and I have to admit it was tempting—under the circumstances—to walk, make that, ride, on the wild side. Thankfully, soundness of mind prevailed.

Nevertheless, the speedometer did seem to inch higher than it should have at certain moments—attributable, no doubt, to the sense of empowerment that comes from being a member of a select class. And so it was that a "bug" could be spotted darting across the Chesapeake Bay Bridge/Tunnel in blatant defiance of the posted speed limit on those Sunday evenings, late, when a certain tired Marine made his mad-dash return to "the reservation" in time for a few hours' shuteye before reveille—after a weekend pass. And so it was too that the volume knob on the radio kept getting cranked clockwise whenever four Leathernecks piled into the car and headed down the highway to take in a Tidewater Tides game.

The VW came through the ordeal unscathed—a phenomenon that can be credited in greater measure to the foresight of German engineering than to the level-headedness of American youth.

Decades have slipped by; now, I am the proud proprietor of a 2001 Chrysler Sebring: officially, "gold," with a Navy blue top, beige leather seats, automatic side-view mirrors, a shiny black steering wheel, power windows, a CD player and flashy chrome rims. Financially, it's a stretch: the dollars that leave the house in order to keep the beauty on the road would be sufficient to run a small generator.

The pros and cons of the matter carefully considered, my feeling is, everyone should be so lucky. All hardworking people of this earth—as a reward for their labors—should have the opportunity to say, as I do:

"Top down…tunes up!"

II. TRAIN WHISTLES

"Listen to the jingle,
the rumble and the roar
As she glides along the woodland
by the hills and by the shore
Hear the mighty rush of the engine,
hear that lonesome hobo's call
We're traveling through the jungle
on the Wabash Cannonball"

"Wabash Cannonball"
Boxcar Willie
Madacy Records, 1995

B orn in a small railroad shack along the "KD line" in Sterrett, Texas, on September 1, 1931, Lecil Travis Martin was destined to become "the world's favorite hobo"—"Boxcar Willie"—a name he took on after writing a song by that title. Although he never developed the flash or sparkle of superstar Country & Western performers like Roy Acuff and Waylon Jennings, "Boxcar Willie," upon turning full-time to singing after an illustrious career in the U.S. Air Force (he logged more than 10,000 hours in the air for Uncle Sam), delighted audiences all over Nebraska and the Dakotas and later England and other parts of the U.S. with his costumed downtrodden look and Hank Williams-like voice. In 1981 he became the sixtieth member inducted into the Grand Ole Opry. He died in Branson, Missouri of leukemia on April 12, 1999.

A commuter-rail train awaits the boarding of passengers before leaving Union Station in Worcester for points east.

> I grew up around trains; they steamed to a stop at
> the railroad station in Union, in the village of Endicott,
> New York. They practically rattled home plate loose at
> one of the ball fields on which I dreamed of becoming
> the next Rocky Colavito. They literally shook the walls
> of the house my friends Dick and Gretchen Boardman
> lived in for a while in nearby Owego. They transport-
> ed me to Eldredge Park in Elmira and Corning Glass
> Works in Corning on school trips when I was a kid. I
> always listened for the whistle, which told me their
> arrival was imminent.

Into life are injected certain sights, sounds, smells and touches
which, in their repeated application, become as integral a part of
the norm as the air we breathe or the water we drink. It is sobering to pause and contemplate the prospective loss of such givens,
were they to be suddenly snatched from our grasp. Take any one
of them away for even the briefest of moments and we would be
rendered rudderless, it appears—or at least cast adrift. We would
be like birds without wings, fish without gills, flowers without
petals.

I have long since grown accustomed to the simultaneously disconcerting and yet reassuring odor of gasoline being drawn from a
pump, for instance. From my earliest days this scent has never been
far from my nostrils, at Cities Service and Texaco and Exxon and
Shell and Sunoco stations the men of my family frequented with their
eight-cylinder cars; it is hard to imagine an existence devoid of a staple that is so thoroughly ingrained in our consciousness.

Other smells are similarly fixed; among them, the aroma of fresh-
baked bread—plump and crusty—of the sort that my maternal
grandmother, Blanche Blossom, used to pull from the oven with mit-
ten-covered hands.

We take for granted the images we can see on a regular basis: school-crossing guards; traffic lights; stop signs. And the objects we can feel with our fingers or toes: a table; a chair; carpeting underfoot.

Then there are the noises all around that serve as ratification that the world is in working order: horns of every kind, including the type—deep and resonant—that carries its message in a series of bursts separated by short lulls over the treetops into every crevice and pocket of town when the Northbridge Fire Department is trying to let people know where an alarm has been sounded.

Similarly, a baby crying from a room or a home not far away, a hammer driving nails as a house undergoes construction or renovation in the neighborhood and a lawnmower whirring loudly outside the kitchen window to signal that grass is being cut are sounds we assume will always be present in our lives. There is no reason to think differently; still, it has been many years since my ears have caught the blast of an air-raid siren—once so routinely struck as a means of conditioning the populace for the possible appearance on the horizon of enemy bombers. Who is to say with any degree of confidence, therefore, that the sounds of yesterday—the whine of a vacuum cleaner, the squeak of sneakers on a basketball court, the rap of a judge's gavel on a court bench, the roar of a crowd, the turn of a key in the lock, the meow of a cat or the bark of a dog—will still be with us tomorrow?

What precipitates this question is the clamor being raised in some parts of the country for eradication of the train whistle, ostensibly in the interest of peace and quiet. Proponents of such a drastic measure are apparently unmoved by all that the train whistle (and the accompanying trail of smoke that wafts across the countryside) symbolizes: development of the western frontier; the progression of commerce to a new level from the time when cargo was carried hither and yon in slow, lumbering fashion by horse and buggy and canal boats; the romanticism of box cars in which hobos found refuge, dining cars in which suave Cary Grant-like characters with cigarettes dangling from their lips wooed beautiful women over glasses of scotch and soda, steel platforms from which conductors yelled "All Aboard!," engine cars from which the man we have come to know as "Casey Jones" waved cheerfully to admirers, and caboose cars whose passage told us that the long and glorious procession was at last coming to an end.

To voluntarily erase such a piece of Americana from the landscape is not only an affront, it is illogical. I could set my watch by the blare of the train whistle to be heard every evening at 9:35 as the Providence & Worcester clatters past on its way south. When those who advocate banning this treasured artifact of a nation's pluck and ingenuity finally lose their fight, as I trust they will, I will be standing by to ask, "What were *you* thinking?"

Mention that I had addressed members of a local business association for forty-five minutes about my career as a journalist and writer prompted Moe Guarini of Rutland, left (with Art Dobson of Shrewsbury), to remark, without a moment's hesitation, "That must have been fiction!" Another time, noticing that a mutual colleague of ours was being carded at the grand opening of a new local restaurant, Moe, who was next in line, asked—with a touch of feigned exasperation in his voice—"What's the drinking age around here, thirty-five?" (He also playfully started to pull his own driver's license, which would have shown him to be in his 50's, from his pocket.) I do not know how many times Moe has delighted me with witty comeuppances of this sort; he is not only a mentor I can trust for sound advice and guidance, he is a person who appreciates that a degree of mirth is essential to happiness. We have shared many pleasant moments as co-workers, in the trenches; I am wealthy beyond measure for being able to say that this kind and gentle soul will be a friend of mine for life.

III. Friends

" 'Cause I've got friends in low places
Where the whiskey drowns
And the beer chases my blues away."

"Friends in Low Places"
Garth Brooks
Capitol Records, 1990

A music impresario and one of the hottest commodities ever to hit the radio airwaves, Garth Brooks (ruler of "Planet Garth" and idol of "GarthNutts" everywhere) was born on February 7, 1962 in Tulsa, Oklahoma. His mother—Colleen Carroll—was a fairly accomplished Country singer. Awarded a track scholarship to Oklahoma State University (he was a skilled javelin thrower), Garth Brooks started performing at clubs in and around Stillwater; his initial stab at establishing himself in Nashville, however, lasted less than a week. And yet he persisted, demonstrating not only a determination to prevail but also a flair for unpredictability that has since manifested itself in such disparate undertakings as a flirtation with professional baseball, a highly publicized break with Capitol Records, "retirement," a commercial association with Wal-Mart and marriage to Trisha Yearwood. His zaniness is exceeded only by his ability to turn out gems: "The Thunder Rolls;" "If Tomorrow Never Comes;" "Standing Outside The Fire;" "She's Every Woman;" "We Shall Be Free;" "American Honky-Tonk Bar Association;" "Ain't Going Down ('Til the Sun Comes Up)"; "Much Too

Young (To Feel This Damn Old)." With the release of his first album, "Garth Brooks," in April of 1989, and then the single "The Dance," which became an immediate sensation, his career began to skyrocket. Before long, fueled by an on-stage aura that was electric in its intensity, Garth Brooks was performing before huge crowds in such far-flung venues as Dublin, Central Park and Texas Stadium. The rest, as they say, is history.

> **The self-pity that Garth Brooks alludes to in "Friends in Low Places" is a common malady, as is the cure prescribed: a man's encounter with a former lover in a social setting leads him to speculate that "I just don't belong" and to assert that "I didn't mean to cause a big scene;" in his despair he reaches for another drink. Initially apologetic, he later turns suddenly unremorseful as his fortitude is steeled by the liquid courage he holds in his hand—and the apparent moral support from his pals—that is readily available to him. "I'll be okay," he says, and then, "I'll head back to the bar and you can kiss my ass." Like Garth Brooks, I cannot imagine a life without friends; in "low," or high, places. To quote Hank Williams Jr., "all my rowdy friends are here for Monday night!"**

A few good friends enrich what might otherwise be a dull and dismal day; multiply the number by ten or twenty or a hundred and the possibilities for a satisfying life are endless. I have found this to be true, and would no sooner think of facing a new dawn without friends than I would consider climbing aboard a bicycle that has no pedals. Friends, in my view, are essential to healthy living; as crucial an element to equilibrium as icing on the cake, oil in the crankcase, ink in the pen.

Genuine friendship is based on reciprocity; he who gives of himself must feel that the commitment is being returned in equal proportion—and vice versa. Unless the match actually ignites the coals, a fire that builds and endures will not follow. "One-way friendships"—and they do exist—are far less rewarding than those in which warm regard is a constant, flowing back and forth: a flame that no sudden rush of wind can extinguish.

In looking at one's circle of friends, it will undoubtedly become apparent that they are "different" in almost every sense of the word: one may be a liberal, another a conservative; one a "party animal," another a wallflower; one wealthy, another poor; one a collector, another a disposer; one an optimist, another a pessimist; one a laugher, another a crier; one a doer, another a slacker. It does not matter; the only determinant worth considering is a friend's affection for you, and yours for him.

Regardless of whether they are handsome or ugly, sharp or dim-witted, smooth or clumsy, civil or uncouth, irrespective of whether they make their living as doctors or ditch diggers, people become friends because of the mutual affinity that dominates. Neither is it of any concern what others think of your fondness for your friends; they could be virtual outcasts in the eyes of some "judges" (i.e., people who view themselves as infinitely superior, but are in truth just average). To maintain an open and sincere friendship in defiance of the pressure to abandon it that is placed on you by those who disapprove is the mark of an individual whose allegiance to a friend cannot be compromised.

In light of this, all petty incidentals that could be construed as potentially disabling to the friendship should be tossed overboard—in order for the bond to remain firmly in place.

The branches of a friendship are invariably rooted in a spark that flew during an initial introduction, or a sharing of interests or hobbies; in many instances, however, friendship springs from nothing more than an inkling that much is to be gained by moving the wagon forward. When this instinct proves correct and the relationship starts to gather momentum, one's sense of gratification is great—providing further impetus to the effort, as acquaintances-turned-friends proceed along the road together.

History has offered up as evidence any number of friendships that seemed to be bound for an irreparable breach at some juncture only to survive and even grow into models deserving of replication. Typical was the friendship between Thomas Jefferson and John Adams: men who helped forge a nation, men who put aside disagreements—even recriminations cast in each other's direction in the heat of argument—to remain comrades for life.

Author David McCullough, in his biography of Adams, John Adams, notes that their correspondence by letters between Monticello and Quincy spanned decades. When Jefferson, suffering from ills that would prove to be fatal, wrote to Adams in March of 1826 (with a plaster copy of an Adams bust looking on from a nearby shelf) to say that his grandson, Thomas Jefferson Randolph, was en route to New England, he added that if the young man did not get to see Adams, it would be as though he had "seen nothing."

Adams's and Jefferson's was a friendship that lasted until they drew their dying breaths, mere hours apart. Jefferson passed at approximately one o'clock in the afternoon on July 4, 1826. Adams passed at 6:20 p.m.

This is the way of friends, that they should share hopes and dreams, confidences and ideas, plans and schemes—even unto the final hour.

Ed Bourgault, a partner in a CPA firm in Worcester (he is pictured with Linda Elie of the Custom Frame Shop in West Boylston at a luncheon) harbors a fondness for tree frogs. "They're so cute," he said as he caught the sound of their chortles during a round of golf we shared in September of 2006. The truth is, Ed has encountered few animals, children or adults he doesn't like; as president of the North Worcester Business Association (NWBA), he regularly rubs elbows with all sorts of people who are integrally involved with the flow of commerce in his favorite city. That he has no enemies should come as no shock; nice guys seldom do!

Marlene Bosma has turned the family's historic barn in Douglas into a flea marketplace that is known far and wide as a spot to find treasures for the home and yard—and hospitality and warmth that refresh the spirit. Amid the antiques and collectibles, at the breakfast and lunch counter and in the tearoom and tavern, signs of welcome are a constant. None of this would have materialized were it not for the energy, vision and commitment Marlene brings to "the show." Lovely and talented (she plays the piano and sings, and in her prime was a jitterbugging sensation), her success as a forward-thinking, hard-nosed entrepreneur is exceeded only by her loyalty to those she calls friends.

His aplomb as an interior designer, decorator, conversationalist, gracious host and independent merchant are pleasingly reflected within the confines of a gentlemen's clothing store Rocco Froio of Charlton (left) operates in Worcester (with Rocco is Alvarez, a handyman and painter who helped put the store together). A framed line drawing of Al Pacino here, an antique typewriter and antique telephone there, silk ties hung like ducks in a row and a sofa strategically positioned to accept garments—casually tossed—or visitors— warmly welcomed—are just a few of the trappings to be found at "Rocco's." Then there are the shoes and sweaters smartly juxtaposed on a wooden table, an umbrella resolutely standing watch in the corner (as if on guard duty), bottles of wine, a pipe rack, a replica ship at full sail, an acoustic guitar, coins scattered on a stand, a hat hung from a full-length mirror and a bottle of Rocco's own cologne occupying a spot on the big desk in the middle of the space that serves as both office and main showroom. Sinatra songs and coffee are a regular embellishment as is talk, and the conversation rivals in pedigree any to be encountered in a barbershop or a golf-course grillroom. The chatter has been known to involve a lawyer, a doctor, a saloon keeper, a journalist, a wine distributor—sometimes individually, sometimes in groups if they all happen to drop by at the same moment. Topics covered range from home maintenance to international travel and cooking. Rocco himself alternately serves as confidante, advisor, teacher, inquisitor and pontificator. Typically the discourse is interrupted only by the jangle of the telephone; when it rings, Rocco, ever the courteous son of dutiful Italian parents, says, "excuse me, please," before answering. What makes Rocco special to his friends is a sense on their part that, even if they never purchased an item of apparel from him, they are always welcome in his shop. Good breeding spawns good people!

Crusader, environmentalist, advocate, real-estate mogul and businesswoman are just a few of the titles that could be assigned to Beth Proko of Worcester. Whether working to restore an historic local park, lobbying for the cleanup of a prominent lake that is situated in her neighborhood, helping to beautify a schoolyard or spearheading efforts to rejuvenate a war memorial that has fallen into disrepair, she brings passion, verve, style and commitment to the cause. Her determination to see a project through to completion regardless of the hurdles that must be cleared has earned Beth high praise from admirers, including state and city officials. When she calls, people respond with materials and labor. When she springs into action, the job gets done. If Beth had been calling the shots, Rome could have been built in a day!

No one could have known with any degree of certainty what assets Barbara Clifford, right (pictured here with restaurateurs Jon and Linda Cohen) would bring with her when she accepted the position of executive director of the Corridor Nine Area Chamber of Commerce in Westborough in 2001. Immediately, however, it became obvious that the organization had gained the services of a fireball. Barbara's electric personality, tirelessness and buoyant advocacy on behalf of "the mission" generated prompt, positive results; membership soared, as did the Chamber's prestige. When Barbara pushes, mountains move!

My world brightened as if a giant light bulb had been turned on the day I met Marty Pratte of Leicester (second from the right in this gathering of colleagues from the *Telegram & Gazette* at a surprise sixtieth birthday party held for me in October of 2005). Marty is merriment on the prowl; whether playing the number 54 in a game of keno, tooling around the lake in his pontoon boat, firing his potato gun in his yard, holding a rummage sale at his desk, shouting "take the blue one!" from the back of the room when a co-worker strides forward to claim a prize in a company sales contest or encouraging male associates to wear a Superman shirt for Halloween, Marty enlivens every occasion. A thousand Martys and the planet would be in far better shape. Pictured from the left are Jay Valencourt, myself, Luisa Heffernan, Moe Guarini (who's getting a bear hug from, who else?, Marty Pratte!) and Chris Grubert.

Acquaintances shudder in apprehension when Chris Liazos of Worcester inquires, as he often does, "Do you want to buy a restaurant?" It isn't the prospective asking price that causes their knees to quiver and their heads to spin, although the mere thought of what it would take to purchase a dining establishment as revered as the Webster House, in Worcester, is enough to make strong souls blanche. It is rather the contemplation of anyone other than Chris being in charge. Customer-oriented and community-minded, and always eager to spread cheer, he is as integral an ingredient in the success of the restaurant as Helena Liazos' famous pies or any of the entrees that come out of the kitchen. Chris pulls no rank as owner; at any given moment he can be seen seating customers, waiting on them, adjusting the room temperature, peddling drinks or clearing tables. His stature as the city's most involved restaurateur has been well earned, and is richly deserved.

I remember being totally mesmerized by the showmanship exhibited by John DiPietro of Holden the first time I saw him in action as chief greeter at a meeting of the Worcester Regional Chamber of Commerce's "Breakfast Club." John is the ultimate people person, which makes him an emcee of the highest caliber. He is the incurable optimist, which makes him an asset to family, friends and business acquaintances. Here he is shown playfully covering up the face of "the other DePetro"—John DePetro of WRKO Radio (680 AM) in front of a poster promoting the station's talk-show heavy hitters at the South Shore Music Circus in Cohasset. "The other DePetro" was subsequently fired by WRKO for slurring gubernatorial candidate Grace Ross, on air; "my John" soldiers on, confident of his abilities as a marketing and public relations impresario and motivational speaker, and as an entertainer. He counts among his cronies Country singing legend Kenny Rogers and Mike Love of The Beach Boys. They, like me, find him to be an irresistibly charming presence!

No one has demonstrated a stronger allegiance to the town of Northbridge, the Massachusetts Republican Party and his family and friends than Harry Berkowitz. A student of civilization, Harry never relents in his attempts to develop a keener understanding of the world around him; by reading voraciously, by immersing himself in PBS and the History Channel and by conversing with others, he has become one of the most learned persons I know. Affectionately dubbed "The Mayor of Rockdale" because of the attachment he has for the neighborhood in which he grew up (and still calls home), Harry would have made a great state rep—had he chosen to pursue a path that leads to that elected office. He possesses one of the great laughs of all time; it is every bit as rollicking and infectious as that of Phyllis Diller or Eddie Murphy. Harry's laugh surfaces often: the mark of a man who is happy to the tips of his toes.

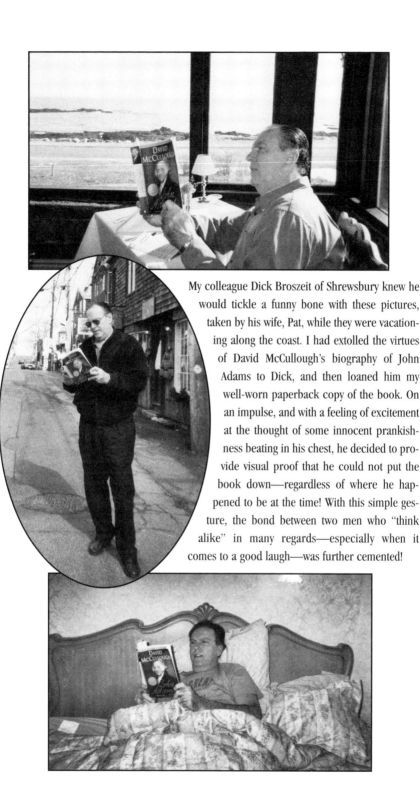

My colleague Dick Broszeit of Shrewsbury knew he would tickle a funny bone with these pictures, taken by his wife, Pat, while they were vacationing along the coast. I had extolled the virtues of David McCullough's biography of John Adams to Dick, and then loaned him my well-worn paperback copy of the book. On an impulse, and with a feeling of excitement at the thought of some innocent prankishness beating in his chest, he decided to provide visual proof that he could not put the book down—regardless of where he happened to be at the time! With this simple gesture, the bond between two men who "think alike" in many regards—especially when it comes to a good laugh—was further cemented!

He is known around the office as "the Stumeister," "the Hermanator," "Stu-eee," "bro," "buddy" or "my friend." An institution at the *Telegram & Gazette*, Stu Herman reciprocates the nicknames he has been accorded by colleagues with affectionate ones for them. These monikers are coined by a man with a personality that never ceases to surprise in what seems to bystanders to be an innocent, childlike play for attention: thus, Liz Vadenais is "Loca Lady" because of her fondness for Ricky Martin; Karen Aloia is "Aloha;" Lynne Ahlberg is "Ah-bug;" the women in Graphics are "Angel Keegan," "Angel Nealon," "Angel Ente" and "Angel Greene;" Veronica Wells and Luisa Heffernan, in Special Sections, are "the two Starlets." And so it goes. Stu reserves feigned disdain for the individual in the building whom he actually holds in highest regard; hence Jay Valencourt is derisively addressed as "The Punk." As such, Jay is subjected to every scrutiny—and every insult—imaginable; and yet, because of the warmth with which the barbs are delivered, it is obvious that these taunts are not poisoned arrows after all but rather terms of endearment. Anyone who demonstrates the least deference toward Jay is, by extension, also deemed a "punk;" Gary Barth, Paul Dinsdale and Mark Dupuis enjoy the dubious distinction of falling into this category. Unmarried, largely self-educated and entirely comfortable in the hustle and bustle of the city, Stu is a world traveler with a vast knowledge of airports, bus stations, nightspots, out-of-town newspapers and "the sights." He is one of the most intriguing people I have ever met and, by virtue of both his kind heart and his zany instincts, a genuine "character."

If ideas were an earthquake, Greg Mangan of Westborough would be at the very epicenter; when his mind starts turning, eruptions come frequently and with an intensity that sends tremors rippling through a room. Even as newspaper people failed to grasp the massiveness of the threat other forms of communication were posing to their livelihood, Greg was arguing that print media needed to rely more heavily on the Internet to attract and retain readers. "Newspapers have a golden opportunity to expand on the reputation they've already achieved as information providers by using the Internet to obtain profiles of their subscribers and to do a better job of furnishing them with the news they want," he said, in 2006. Unfortunately, the ears of those to whom his remarks were addressed weren't listening; even as, to put it in Greg's own words, "the truck was heading off the cliff." At other times, Greg has lobbied for the worthiness of a book that would explore the intriguing ramifications of relocating the United Nations to Jerusalem; he has also pitched the concept of a computerized frequent diner's card that would provide restaurants with a snapshot of their customers' culinary habits and tastes when it is swiped as they come through the door, and of a web site that is dedicated to establishing "term limits" for senators and representatives. Greg shows no discouragement when his proposals do not receive an enthusiastic embrace; he simply keeps dipping his cup into the well for more! A mind IS a terrible thing to waste; in Greg's case, there is no danger that such a calamity will occur.

Sylvester Martin had just begun his shift tending the Salvation Army bucket outside the Walgreen's on Park Avenue in his adopted city of Worcester twelve days before Christmas, 2006 when he was unceremoniously interrupted. I was looking for a photo that would consummately capture the essence of my chapter on "Life." "I'm originally from Indianapolis, Indiana," he said. "I'm a Hoosier!" No one appreciates the life-sustaining work done throughout the year by the Salvation Army better than Sylvester. "Coming from a poverty-stricken family myself, I know that the Salvation Army does a lot of good work," he said. "I don't know what people would do without the Salvation Army."

IV. Life

"We didn't start the fire
It was always burning
Since the world's been turning…"

"We Didn't Start The Fire"
Billy Joel
Columbia Records, 1989

I f the career of Billy Joel were defined by one song (as Kate Smith's was, and Ronan Tynan's is, by "God Bless America"), the obvious choice would be "Piano Man," not "We Didn't Start The Fire." Hearing "Piano Man" today, more than three decades after Billy Joel recorded it in Los Angeles, sends shivers up and down my spine. "Piano Man" is Billy Joel's masterpiece; the picture he draws of "John at the bar" who is "quick with a joke, or to light up your smoke," of Paul who is "a real-estate novelist," and of Davey "who's still in the Navy and probably will be for life," is as apt a rendering of "businessmen sharing a drink they call loneliness" as has ever been produced in a short burst of verse. The concluding lines infuse the sketch with a final dash of color: "And the piano sounds like a carnival/and the microphone smells like a beer/and they sit at the bar and put bread in my jar/and say, 'Man, what are you doing here?' " With these words, "Piano Man" is ready to be hung on the wall, for keeps, as if it were a Van Gogh painting or an Ansel Adams photograph. "Piano Man" secured Billy Joel's place in the pantheon populated by the icons of Pop; and yet that track is but a single example of his brilliance as a lyricist and a singer. That he has also been a semi-tragic figure, haunted by bouts of depression and occasional battles with alcohol and drugs, only serves to heighten his allure to his fans, and to make his numerous triumphs that much more remarkable. And the successes are something to behold: the songs, "Allentown," "Uptown Girl," "You're Only Human (Second Wind)," "Just the Way You Are," "The River of Dreams," for example; and the albums, "52nd Street," "Glass Houses" and, more recently, "My Lives," among the most prominent. Little wonder then that worldwide sales of his records surged past one hundred million in 1999, or that he has earned induction into both the Songwriters Hall of Fame and the Rock & Roll Hall of Fame, or that he has received a Grammy Legend Award, or that the Broadway musical "Movin' Out" is grounded in his music. On top of this Billy Joel's basic decency has made him an endearing character. His enthusiasm for supporting charitable causes does not wane. His belief in the merits of music education is unwavering; it has taken him from one school to another as a guest speaker. Still there is a restlessness that commands that more be done; hence the launch of the Long Island Boat Company, a Billy Joel exclusive! But, whether singing solo or in collaboration with Don Henley, Sting or Elton John, it's ultimately about the music. As Billy Joel himself put it in his first No. 1 single, "It's Still Rock N Roll to Me."

Billy Joel's "We Didn't Start The Fire" is a song that ponders the proverbial march of time, seemingly resolute and unstoppable. It always gets my blood racing, and the wheels of my mind turning.

Round and round the earth revolves and with this rotation—so methodical in its spin that it is taken for granted—the days of a man's life are shaped by the events and people of his time. What comes before and after is of no less import in an historical context; nevertheless, the here and now assumes its rightful place as the predominant yardstick by which a man measures the length and breadth of the years.

Having been born into an "Eisenhower household" in 1945 as the son of a carpenter and a homemaker, neither of whom enjoyed the benefits of an education that extended beyond the ninth grade, I was presented with a set of stimuli unique to my circumstances. These prods to some extent shaped my future course: my parents voted Republican; my grandfathers and uncles were all tradesmen; family gatherings occurred frequently and perpetuated a strong bond between myself and my cousins and other relatives; the neighborhood in which I grew up was relatively new and so was the television in our living room; the TV programs we watched, all in black and white, included "Ozzie and Harriet," "Father Knows Best," "The Honeymooners," "The Lawrence Welk Show," "Wyatt Earp," "The Ted Mack Amateur Hour," "Mr. Ed," "The Ed Sullivan Show" and "The Game of the Week" (narrated by Dizzy Dean and his sidekick Pee Wee Reese). These programs promulgated an atmosphere of benign acceptance of the status quo (why change a good thing?).

This innocuous environment reached beyond my immediate perimeter for miles in all directions; this in turn afforded assurance that I would probably not stray down "the wrong path."

And yet it was not long afterwards that a far more provocative array of influences rumbled into view, turning my life upside down. Billy Joel, a contemporary of mine, had experienced similar upheaval in a world apparently gone mad. He captured the essence of this continual chaos in his song "We Didn't Start The Fire." In 1956, he noted, there was "Bardot, Budapest, Alabama, Khrushchev;" the images of these phenomena—a sex pot/pinup girl, an uprising, racial chaos and a tempestuous Communist bent on literally "burying" the West—stir the adrenalin even now. Come '63, Billy Joel pointed out, there was "J.F.K. blown away, what else do I have to say." To live through the assassination of a beloved president—to witness, in fact, the entire drama play out over and over again on the very screens that had only shortly before carried such tame scenes as Jack Benny pretending he couldn't play the violin (for laughs), or Roy Rogers and Dale Evans singing

"Happy Trails"—was to realize with an increasing sense of foreboding and despair that our "Life of Riley" was gone, never to return.

And then, between '64 and '89, Billy Joel says, came a new wave of disconcerting developments to cause further distress; among them, "Foreign Debts, Homeless Vets, AIDS, Crack, Bernie Goetz."

It is no wonder, having addressed a plethora of ingredients starting with "Harry Truman, Doris Day, Red China, Johnnie Ray" in '49 (the year William Martin Joel was born) and ending (for the moment) with "Rock and Roller Cola Wars" in '89, he asserts, as if figuratively throwing his hands up in the air, "...I can't take it anymore."

But in suggesting in one breath that "it's always been burning" in this fashion since the beginning of the universe and then wondering in the next whether "...when we are gone/will it still burn on, and on, and on...," he answers his own question: from the age of dinosaurs and Neanderthals, Cain and Abel, David and Goliath, Moses, Socrates, Plato, Shakespeare, William the Conqueror, Balboa, Blackbeard, Rembrandt, Einstein and Robert Burns right on through to the appearance in the headlines of Pearl Harbor, Mike Tyson, the U.S.S. Cole, Paris Hilton, chat rooms, Ipods, space trips to Pluto, hanging chads, a tsunami, Hurricane Katrina, Monica Lewinsky, Eric Rudolph, a whale in the Thames, Princess Di, global warming, Howard Stern, Denzel Washington, Donald Trump, "American Idol," Ariel Sharon, Michael Jackson, Sharon Stone, Madonna and of course 9/11, the flame has not flickered. It was lit eons ago by an entity mightier than any single human act or any random event; it transcends all earthly bounds; it defies rational explanation even while continuing to enthrall and mystify; it started with a spark mere mortals are helpless to effectively describe; it will end with a bang the magnificence of which no engineer, scientist or seer can sufficiently foretell.

"We" didn't start the fire. "We" won't extinguish it, either.

V. FAITH

"Oh Lord my God
When I in awesome wonder
Consider all the worlds
Thy hands have made…"

"How Great Thou Art"
Elvis Presley
RCA Victor Records, 1967

For every action there is a reaction. When Elvis Aaron Presley burst onto the music scene in the 1950s, teenagers flipped in delight. Parents, however, recoiled in horror. Warning notes were sounded by elders: "He is the devil incarnate;" "He will corrupt America's youth;" "He confirms our worst suspicions about this new craze called Rock & Roll." Elvis, of course, was nothing of the sort; the U.S. Jaycees named him one of the ten outstanding young men in the nation in 1970! Born into humble circumstances in Tupelo, Mississippi on January 8, 1935, Elvis Presley used his God-given talents to become the matinee idol of a generation. Endowed with a voice as pure as mountain spring water and disarming good looks, he blended these assets together with gyrations and gestures and facial expressions to create an aura the world had never seen. Appearances in thirty-three films, on television, in TV specials and in live shows coupled with a highly publicized stint in the U.S. Army cemented the adoration his ever-growing legion of fans felt for him. My mother, who loved to dance, and who'd been accustomed to listening to the mellow strains of Tommy Dorsey, Guy Lombardo, Glenn Miller and Count Basie as a young woman, became

If there is one thing that New England has in abundance, it is magnificent churches. They can be found along main streets and back roads alike, firmly planted on flatlands and hilltops and rising in stately fashion toward the heavens. Crafted of wood, brick or stone, they are an architectural marvel. They never fail to take the breath away.

a convert! It wasn't until Elvis Presley fell prey to the same temptations that have done in other great artists that he lost his way. But he was never a threat to bring down the young; the only life he ruined, as he became a parody of himself and ultimately a model for thousands of woeful copycat Elvises, was his own. And no one loved his Lord more, onto the end. I recently purchased a 25th-anniversary (1955-1980) limited-edition set of Elvis records that is every Elvis-admirer's dream come true: eight discs, consisting of an early live performance with a monlogue, an early benefit performance, collectors' gold from the movie years, the TV specials, the Las Vegas years, lost singles, Elvis at the piano/the concert years (Part I) and the concert years/concluded. On no song does Elvis reach deeper into himself than on "How Great Thou Art." Those who have disparaged Elvis are wrong; he was an American original and an entertainer and musician who had no equal. He was also a believer, as his frequent forays into Gospel proved. He was, and always will be, "the King."

Images of my grandmother, Blanche Blossom, playing "The Old Rugged Cross" on the piano, and singing along, are still as fresh in my mind as the mix of dread and excitement I felt the Sunday morning I was baptized; memories of West Endicott Baptist Church and summer weeks spent in Bible camp at Lake Arrowhead and Easter sunrise services and "Pastor Dick" playing the tambourine at Whitinsville United Methodist Church are still vivid too. I do not attend church regularly these days. But I am still a Christian.

It does not diminish my esteem for churchgoers at all that I am no longer one of them. Indeed, the ultimate test of a born-again Christian's faith may be how he conducts his life without the sustaining influence of the sanctuary. For just as it is in the encounter with a steep and slippery slope that a mountain climber discovers whether his skills and resolve are up to the challenge, so it is in a rendezvous with temptation—hour after hour, day after day—that a believer learns whether his spirituality is genuine or artificial.

Some who pay due homage to the requirements of their religion would contend that it is a copout to suggest that adherence to pre-scribed tenets, practices and dictates can be scrupulously maintained independent of the sacraments. Let them think what they will; my own experience has convinced me that Sunday-morning worship is not a prerequisite to "walking the straight and narrow."

A person can fairly judge only from a comparison of the two approaches; having been raised as a Baptist (and in fact immersed in the waters of redemption as a young boy), it was perfectly natural for me to assume that sliding my way into a pew—dutifully scrubbed to a sheen, Bible in hand—was going to be the path of choice until that moment at which I would no longer be able, physically, to do so. For a long time I took it for granted that this weekly dose of prayer, hymn singing, Scripture reading, pledging and sermonizing to which I so willingly (and sometimes not so eagerly) submitted would continue—as each new Sabbath rolled around—unto death. Very recently, and quite abruptly, I have ended the habit: for reasons, entirely of a selfish nature, that no regular worshipper would embrace as acceptable. Nevertheless, except for the profound sense of shame I feel for having done so whenever I think about my nonparticipation in the ordered methodology, I am none the worse for the decision—in my opinion, at least. I have not been struck down by lightning; I have not bedded the seductress; the sky has not fallen.

Ralph Waldo Emerson underwent a similar "turning." In his biography of "the Sage of Concord," entitled *Emerson/The Mind on Fire,* Robert D. Richardson Jr. notes that Emerson—son of a minister and himself seemingly destined for a career in the pulpit—suddenly and resoundingly shed his clerical robe (the path "ordained" by the hierarchy as the correct course) in favor of a more individualized approach. In his famous "Divinity School Address" of July 15, 1838, Emerson, then just thirty-five years of age, rejected the notion of "formal historical Christianity"—recommending instead a "personal religious consciousness." Emerson had come to the conclusion that the light that burns inside is the most accurate gauge of a person's worthiness in the eyes of God, and that a structured formula, as devised by man, was not necessary to the attainment of absolution.

To receive revelation from another, "when pure Heaven was pouring itself into each of us, on the simple condition of obedience," was itself an irreverent means to an end, Emerson said. "To listen to any second-hand gospel is perdition of the first gospel. Jesus was Jesus because he refused to listen to another, and listened at home," Emerson said.

Setting aside for the time being the hypocrisy I have found to be so rampant within the ranks of organized religion (there is the married Methodist pastor I knew who skipped town after having an affair with the church secretary, and Catholic priests' abuse of mere innocents, for instance—and their superiors' decision to cover it up), I feel, as Emerson did, that an exemplary existence is one in which "good" (as opposed to "evil") is pursued with such vigor that it takes over a person's entire soul. The real Christian is the one who meets the Creator not on man's terms but on his own, through a variety of exposures, and who, as a consequence, lets these raptures prevail. In my case it is by clutching to my bosom the privilege of drawing breath—a privilege like no other; of knowing, too, that there is a higher purpose to life than consumption, rudimentary motions and repose.

I am aware of a great many Christians for whom church is the foundation of a life to be celebrated because of its purity, starting with my maternal grandmother, Blanche Blossom. I realize, also, that there is a contradiction at work in that I derive much of the inspiration for my own faith from efforts produced by man in his attempts to glorify God; this explains why I can be lifted by voices raised to the rafters in blissful harmony by the Bill Gaither singers on television on Saturday evenings, by the poetry of Wordsworth, by the writings of Norman Vincent Peale or William F. Buckley Jr., by the preaching of Billy Graham, by the witnessing of Mother Theresa, by the sacrifice of

Schindler or Anne Frank. I am no more firmly connected to my God than when I am reading "The Beatitudes" in Luke, Chapter 6, indulging in quiet meditation, or listening to such powerful lures as "Amazing Grace," by George Jones, "Take My Hand, Precious Lord," by Elvis Presley, or "Turn Your Radio On," by The Jordanaires.

Still, the stronger persuasions—the ones that provoke incredulity, and a deep and abiding conviction that all is well—are those delivered directly from His hand: sunrises and sunsets, rainbows, clouds, stars, snowfalls, nighttime, downpours, tides, rivers, creeks, wind, trees, birds, insects, animals, eclipses, meteors, birth, death, Earth. And miracles.

These are the posts to which the ropes of my ship are tethered; they are bound tight, with or without the church as the decisive guiding force.

VI. Boxing

"Don't give us none
of your aggravation
We had it with your discipline
Saturday night's alright for fighting
Get a little action in"

"Saturday Night's Alright for Fighting"
Elton John
MCA Records, 1973

*B*orn Reginald Kenneth Dwight on March 25, 1947 in a suburb of *London, Elton John was a child prodigy on the piano; tutored in the classics, he did not make any secret of his love for Rock 'N' Roll. He would ultimately shake the world of music to its core not only with his brilliance as a songwriter and performer but with his work ethic, his showmanship and his versatility. He has produced one chart-topping hit after another and has sold millions upon millions of singles and albums including "Candle in the Wind 1997" written in memory of his friend Princess Diana. His devotion to causes, such as a research and cure for AIDS, knows no bounds. "The Rocket Man" is a towering talent for whom even the sky is not the limit.*

Boxing has provided America with shining moments. There was Joe Louis's destruction of Max Schmeling. There was the friendship that emerged from the legendary fights between Jack Dempsey and Gene Tunney. There was the cockiness of Cassius Clay

The courage that is the hallmark of the pugilist is reflected in the eyes of both trainer Carlos Garcia and his protégé, Jose Antonio Rivera, on fight night. Together, in and out of the ring, they have shared exhilarating highs and demoralizing lows while bringing pride to the city they call "home." Like Rivera, who rose to world-class status under Garcia's tutelage, youngsters continue to gravitate to the Boys & Girls Club in Worcester; there, Garcia, in the fashion of a dutiful father, dispenses advice and guidance that turns weaklings into warriors and novices into aces. On this particular afternoon, Garcia's gym was awash with children (and one mother, who, in pondering whether to sign her son up for the program, asked such questions as, "He will always wear headgear, right?").

just after he won an Olympic gold medal. Boxing has also left the nation scarred and at times tainted. Purists, however, will never accept the premise that its periodic descent into absurdity leaves the sport with no redeeming value. Nor should they.

The assumption by so many who disparage the sport that has come to be known as "the ancient art of self-defense" and in its most intimate quarters as "The Sweet Science" is that its practitioners are principally motivated by a proclivity for violence. Were that truly the case, the blood, and death, would flow in a torrent of ghastly dimensions: on a scale, even, of gore produced by cockfights or war.

It is not so difficult either to proceed from this theory that pugilists are nothing more than barbarians—their loin cloths exchanged for silk trunks—to the conclusion that those who stream into auditoriums and halls and arenas to sit as observers of the mayhem are themselves only a step above Neanderthals. "Do not misjudge," is the prevailing senti-ment: the ones attired in tuxedos and gowns, as if in readiness for a night at the opera, or a viewing of Oklahoma! on Broadway, are pos-sessed of sadistic tendencies every bit as deplorable as those exhibited by the combatants they so ardently encourage.

Hence the occasional clamor for abolition of the craft, for the same reason a civilized society bans duels at twenty paces or games of "chicken" involving automobiles racing towards each other, head-on: the objective being, in outlawing such waywardness, to maintain a sense of decorum.

In their fervor to eradicate an evil from the face of the planet, haters of boxing choose to ignore the factors that compel men (and now women) to undergo the rigors of training and the savagery of the ring in the first place. In their estimation, "the dance of two warriors" has no redeeming qualities; there is only the spectacle of unsavory promoters, "thrown" matches, the ever-looming threat of the onset of Parkinson's disease and a vanquished fighter flat on his back on the canvas—a physician detecting no quiver of movement and indeed no pulse—to consider. The cry goes, "In the name of all that is decent, for the sake of our very existence as a community of mature adults, we must ban this infantilism."

I beg to disagree. In its purest form, unshackled of the leg irons that hinder its capacity to walk in glory, boxing deserves not rebuke but honor. Boiled to its essence, boxing represents an individual's struggle to overcome inner doubt, to rise above circumstance and fear, to bring himself to a state of physical perfection and poise, and ultimately to prove one's courage—win, lose or draw.

This is what I absorb from studying the people who have populated the sport since its beginnings: the trainers and handlers and managers and commentators and referees and judges and cut men and boxing writers: a sometimes-beleaguered fraternity that is nevertheless proud of the fight game's unmistakable value as a means to determine a person's mettle—mentally, physically and emotionally.

It is a vocation that has given rise to various and sundry co-habitants: the assemblers of *Ring* magazine, which has long been recognized as "the bible" of the sport; the analysts (the Howard Cosells, Larry Merchants and Teddy Atlases of the airwaves); the famed trainers (Cus D'Amato and Angelo Dundee come immediately to mind); the fabulous settings in which the legendary battles have been waged (Madison Square Garden, the Los Angeles Coliseum, Caesar's Palace); the ring announcers, their voice asking in a plaintiff blare that slices through the darkness of night, "Are you ready to rumble?," or declaring, in the glimmer of the floodlights, "It's Showtime!" (Michael Buffer and Jimmy Gleason Jr., respectively); the celluloid heroes whose roles on the silver screen capture the heart and the soul of formidable fighters (Sylvester Stallone as "Rocky Balboa" ranking as the most obvious example), and of course the champions who have come and gone, whose names evoke images of men able to bob and weave and feint and uppercut and backpedal and "slip" and jab and counter and punch and shuffle, as if imbued with powers that are beyond a mortal's comprehension: Jack Johnson; Archie Moore; Joe Louis; Harry Krebs; Sugar Ray Leonard;

Khiary Gray, 14, looking every bit like a future Winky Wright or Zab Judah, pummels the speed bag during a training session at the Worcester Boys & Girls Club.

Ed Suyer of Worcester works the heavy bag at Gold's Gym in Westborough on July 18, 2006. "I help the guys who box here train, and spar," he said. For all who love the sport, the compulsion to engage in "the ancient art of self-defense" is as instinctive as the urge to eat or drink. The rewards, too, are just as great.

James Braddock; Rocky Marciano; Marvin Hagler; Jack Dempsey; Joe Frazier; Carmen Basilio; Oscar de la Hoya; Floyd Patterson; Larry Holmes; George Foreman; Floyd Mayweather; Winky Wright.

God in His foresight has blessed a precious few, when they are young, with the seeming perfect amalgamation of assets: weight, height, reach, hand and foot speed, punching power, intelligence, savvy and will that are so ideally aligned that the rarest of fighters subsequently emerges; a boxer who can not only boast of being able to "float like a butterfly and sting like a bee" but who can deliver the victories and the championship belts that prove it is not just braggadocio. I speak, of course, of Muhammad Ali (formerly known as Cassius Clay, "the Louisville Lip").

The detractors of boxing have it wrong in their premise that people who are infatuated with the sport are drawn to it by a need to witness a gash opened above the eye or a broken nose or any combination of abrasions and swellings and disfigurements and disablements. True followers never desire a maiming (they may hunger for a knockout, or a TKO, but only if the victim is temporarily and not permanently incapacitated). Their preference would be for a battle that is "legit" from the opening bell to the last, in which both combatants demonstrate prowess of extraordinary scope (at a distance, or toe-to-toe) and who then embrace one another in a sign of mutual admiration and respect when it is finished and a decision is rendered.

I have always yearned for a sport that is scrupulously policed, and unsullied by scandal and tragedy; a sport that leaves its participants with their wits intact when their fighting days are done. It is a high-wire act, attempting to achieve this delicate balance that results in a fighter who can dazzle between the ropes and eventually walk away sound of body and mind. It doesn't happen often; when it does, we who cherish fighters for the dedication they bring to their profession bask in the moment.

Unlike the cheap-shot artists, we wait, expectantly, for The Next Big Fight.

New York City father saves student from Mass.

Pair rolled between tracks as train passed over them

By Deepti Hajela
THE ASSOCIATED PRESS

NEW YORK — In hindsight, jumping in front of an oncoming subway train may not have been the smartest move Wesley Autrey has ever made.

"It's all hitting me now," Autrey said yesterday, the day after he saved the life of a young man who had fallen onto the tracks. Autrey pushed him into a gap between the rails. "I'm looking, and these trains are coming in now. ... Wow, you did something pretty stupid."

But even knowing that he had a narrow escape from injury or death, the 50-year-old Harlem construction worker doesn't regret his choice.

"I did something to save someone's life," Autrey said.

The father of three was in the center of a media storm yesterday, lauded for his quick thinking and quicker reflexes, offered rewards for his heroism and even booked to appear on David Letterman's talk show.

Waiting for a downtown Manhattan train on Tuesday, he saw Cameron Hollopeter, a film student, suffering from some kind of medical episode. After stumbling down the platform, Hollopeter, of Littleton, Mass., fell onto the tracks with a train on its way into the station.

Autrey, traveling with his two young daughters, knew he had to do something.

"If I let him stay there by himself, he's going to be dismembered," the Navy veteran remembered thinking.

He jumped down to the tracks, a few feet below platform level, and rolled with the young man into a drainage trough — cold, wet and more than a little unpleasant smelling — between the rails as the southbound No. 1 train came into the 137th Street-City College station.

The train's operator saw someone on the tracks and put the emergency brakes on. Some

THE ASSOCIATED PRESS
Wesley Autrey stands Tuesday with his two daughters Syshe, 4, left, and Shuqui, 6, at the Broadway and 145th Street subway stop in New York.

saved our son's life," dad Larry Hollopeter said, his voice choking up. "There are no words to properly express our gratitude and feelings for his actions."

The unusual rescue with its happy ending brought the media horde to Autrey. He spent the day doing interviews, mainly at his mother's apartment, where his sister Linda had been pressed into service as phone answerer and scheduler.

The phone rang frequently, with calls coming in from all over the country offering rewards as

A newspaper clipping tells the story of Wesley Autrey, a fifty-year-old Harlem construction worker who with hardly a thought for his own welfare jumped in front of an oncoming subway train to save the life of a film student after seeing that the latter had fallen onto the tracks. Facing the pop of flashbulbs and questions from a horde of reporters a day after the spur-of-the-moment rescue, which occurred in January of 2007, Autrey, in a retrospective mood, described his actions as probably "pretty stupid." Others felt differently. The father of the film student, choking back tears, said, "There are no words to properly express our gratitude and feelings" for Autrey's heroism. Autrey's daughters Shuqui, six, and Syshe, four, were traveling with him when the incident happened and thus observed first-hand the sort of bravery that separates a true hero from mere mortals.

VII. HEROES

"And then a hero comes along
With the strength to carry on
And you cast your fears aside
And you know you can survive..."

"Hero"
Mariah Carey
Sony Music, 1993

An apparent lack of ambition suggested that Mariah Carey was seemingly headed nowhere fast as a teenager and young adult. She was nicknamed "Mirage" in high school because she seldom showed up for class. Her initial foray into the working world, which included jobs as a hat/coat check girl, a hair sweeper in salons and a waitress as she struggled to make ends meet, revealed no signs of the commitment it takes to succeed: she was fired repeatedly. She possessed a rare gift, however; from about the age of three she was able to sing and to do so exactly on note and with a range of voice that would later be described as "spectacular." Given her name by her mother (who was white Irish American—her father was black Venezuelan American) from the song "They Call The Wind Mariah," she arrived on the music scene with the wallop of a hurricane and blew the doors down with one No. 1 hit after another. One of these, "One Sweet Day," spent a record sixteen weeks on the Billboard "Hot 100." Her seventeenth No. 1 single tied Mariah with Elvis Presley for second on the all-time list of No. 1's just behind The Beatles and established her as the highest-selling female artist of all time (she has also been touted as one of the world's one-hundred sexiest women).

Instinctively good-hearted, especially when it comes to children, she founded Camp Mariah, in Fishkill, New York—an escape for inner-city youth. At Camp Mariah, urban kids are encouraged to embrace the arts, pursue career paths and to build self-esteem.

I have never understood why people are so reluctant to talk about their heroes. I constantly look to the men and women I have chosen as personal heroes for inspiration, and am not shy in trumpeting their achievements and values to others—in conversation—as a way to acknowledge their pedigree. Instead of hiding heroes under a bushel basket in the basement, we ought to place them on a pedestal in the light. By sharing them with others, we are saying their lives are so exemplary that they merit wide circulation; by proclaiming our devotion to the actions and beliefs of our heroes, we infer that there is in us, perhaps, a little bit of the hero too.

Imagine a world without heroes; a place barren as a desert or the deepest vacuums of space when it comes to any personage that could be held up as an example of the very best instincts humanity can muster: bravery; fortitude; wisdom; compassion; comprehension; selflessness.

God forbid that Earth had been saddled with such a disadvantage from the dawn of civilization! Curse the morning the flatlands and the mountains and the oceans were denied the presence of individuals willing to expend every last drop of blood in the cause of liberty, justice and goodness—had the Creator deemed it appropriate in the beginning that no single being should be accorded the capacity to rise above the tendencies toward which he or she is inclined in emerging from the womb (greed, jealousy, prejudice, deceit)!

What a miserable place to call home, if this were the case!

Given that it is not, it must also be pointed out that we (nations and societies) often ascribe far too loosely the title of hero; and that, as if to compound the error, we all too frequently assign the mantle to those who are least deserving of the honor.

It's interesting that in its primary definitions of the word, Webster's leans towards the premise that a hero must by design be a man: a male, Webster's says, who is admired for his "courage, nobility or exploits, especially in war;" anyone, but "particularly a man," whose attributes or achievements are regarded "as an ideal or model;" and, again, "the central male character in a novel, play, poem, etc., with whom the reader or audience is supposed to sympathize."

These descriptions no doubt emanate from myths passed down through the ages; their origin is buried in Greek legend: a priestess of Aphrodite at Sestos, named Hero, throws herself into the sea in despair after her lover, Leander, drowns in a storm swimming the Hellespont to be with her.

I would argue that, first of all, no documentation culled from the pages of history can be brought forward to support the contention that a global assemblage of heroes is in fact peopled exclusively by men; and that, secondly, the issuance of the rank of hero ought to be a rare occurrence. It should be reserved for the select few who have conspicuously and dramatically exceeded expectations of what the body, heart and soul are able to accomplish during the run of days allotted to them.

Tempting as it is for those of us who are fans of the Fox television show "24" to think of Counter Terrorism Unit (CTU) Agent Jack Bauer (as portrayed by Keifer Sutherland) as a hero, he is only a figment of a writer's imagination (this doesn't stop avid followers of "24" from placing Jack Bauer on a throne reserved for the truly special; in rattling off a list of reasons why Jack Bauer should be considered a superhero, for instance, Radio Talk-Show Host Rush Limbaugh mentioned three that caught my attention: "Superman wears Jack Bauer pajamas;" "When Jack Bauer was in kindergarten, for 'Show and Tell,' he killed a terrorist;" and, "It took Jesus Christ three days to rise from the dead…it took Jack Bauer twenty-four hours, and he's done it twice!").

To me, Eleni Gatzoyiannis is a hero. About this there can be no dispute: the evidence is irrefutable. The story of "Eleni" as told in a book written by her son, Nicholas Gage, and then a movie starring Kate Nelligan and John Malkovich, moves me to tears of appreciation as only an account of the deeds of a living, breathing saint can.

It has been many years since I last watched the film *Eleni*; yet the picture of Eleni Gatzoyiannis standing before a firing squad with her back to a ravine, raising her arms in the air and shouting, "My children!" as she is shot is riveted in my mind. It feeds my continuing conviction that in a world populated by a fair share of tyrants, there is room for genuine heroes.

A victim of civil strife that erupted in Greece following the Second World War, Eleni Gatzoyaiannis—a simple peasant woman from the small, remote village of Lia—reluctantly gave up one of her daughters to fight with the army even though the cause was one she did not understand. For refusing to surrender the rest of her children to be raised as Communists, and in fact adding insult to injury by smuggling four of the five out of the country to America—and freedom—she was subjected to hard labor, tortured and executed. She fell dead at the age of forty-one.

It is fitting and proper that a tribute to motherhood presented by the Women's International Center is called "the Eleni Award."

Like Eleni Gatzoyiannis, true heroes handle adversity, challenge, disappointment and defeat—even hopelessness—with an assurance that whatever the outcome of their travails, a reward awaits. Every word they speak, every idea they formulate, every step they take, every movement they make is showered in a resolute certainty that all will end satisfactorily.

The urge so commonly followed in a time in which artificiality reigns is to proclaim that an athlete is a hero in recognition of his or her skills on the field of competition; or that a prominent actor or actress is a hero in celebration of the luminance he or she brings to the big screen. In neither case are the determinants of particular value in mounting an argument for hero status. Only when their talents are used in total submission to a cause that is bigger than the defined parameters of their endeavor do they become heroes, as Jesse Owens's were in the 1936 Olympics in Berlin. By winning four gold medals at those Games (in the 100 and 200-meter sprints, the running broad jump and as anchorman on the U.S.'s 400-meter relay), Owens defied German Dictator Adolf Hitler's theories of an Aryan "master race;" when it came time to present Owens with his victory medals, Hitler, infuriated, stormed out of the stadium. Or as Jackie Robinson's were in breaking major-league baseball's color barrier in 1947. Like Jesse Owens, Jackie Robinson's athletic brilliance was apparent early on (he was a track, baseball, football and baseball standout in Pasadena, California, growing up, and at UCLA); it was the remarkable restraint he demonstrated in enduring the barbs and taunts that accompanied his wearing of the uniform of the Brooklyn Dodgers, however, that stamped him as a hero.

It's revelatory too that Jesse Owens and Jackie Robinson both went on to success in the corporate world, after retiring from sports.

No touch of cowardice could be detected in the short but exemplary life of Nathan Hale, a true American hero. A young man consumed by patriotism, Nathan Hale was raised on a Connecticut farm, attended Yale and then became a schoolteacher. He and his five brothers all shouldered arms in the cause of liberty. Having served with the Continental Army in the siege of Boston in 1775, he was promoted to the rank of captain and joined the defense of New York City early in 1776. He was just twenty-one years old when he volunteered to run a reconnaissance mission behind enemy lines on Long Island. No one could talk him out of the dangerous task; he was adamant that he still hadn't done enough to help his homeland. Posing as a Dutch schoolmaster, he obtained the desperately needed intelligence he had set out for but was captured by the British as he tried to return to his regiment on Manhattan Island. General Sir William Howe ordered him hung. He died the morning of September 21, 1776.

The fourteen words with which Captain Nathan Hale met his fate are among the most gallant ever spoken: "I only regret that I have but one life to lose for my country."

Heroes have occupied a prominent role in my own personal journey, as I strive to learn from the lessons they have taught. Heroes—past and present—are ever near, whispering encouragement in our ear, if we would only listen.

VIII. BASEBALL

"Well, beat the drum
and hold the phone
the sun came out today!
We're born again,
there's new grass on the field…"

"Centerfield"
John Fogerty
Dreamworks SKG, 1985

J ohn Fogerty's skills as a songwriter and vocalist are undisputable; a founder and the lead singer of the legendary band Creedence Clearwater Revival (CCR), he has authored such classics as "Fortunate Son," "Proud Mary," "Bad Moon Rising," "Born On The Bayou" and "Who'll Stop The Rain." His time with CCR was a tumultuous period, though, leading to a breakup of the group, years of disputes and lawsuits and a lengthy estrangement from the label—Fantasy Records—on which he'd gained fame. He moved on to a solo career that, despite the creation of such minor hits as "Rockin' All Over The World" and "Almost Saturday Night," proved far less satisfactory than his days with CCR. Through it all Fogerty fought for his rights; in one memorable legal case, a claim was made that the chorus of Fogerty's "The Old Man Down The Road" bore too close a resemblance to that of CCR's "Run Through The Jungle." In a splendid display of chutzpah, Fogerty took the witness stand with guitar in hand and played excerpts from both songs to prove that they were different. He won the argument. The personal tragedies that have befallen him, including the loss of his brother and fellow musician Tom Fogerty, who died in September of 1990 after con-

Gary Haddock of the Baltimore Orioles' Event Staff caught my attention as he hawked ballot forms for Major League Baseball's 2006 All-Star Game to fans sitting high in the stands along the right-field line at Camden Yards during a game against the Boston Red Sox on May 17, 2006. Former Red Sox infielder Kevin Millar's two-run homer off knuckleball pitcher Tim Wakefield in the bottom of the fourth staked the Orioles to a 2-1 lead and they went on to win the contest behind the pitching of Erik Bedard, 4-3. The victory snapped a thirteen-game losing streak to Boston—the longest such run of futility in Orioles' club history. Three particular treats for me were seeing Camden Yards for the first time, hearing Orioles fans break into deep-throated chants of "Or-e-ole" and exiting the ballpark through the corridors of the B&O building beyond the outfield fence (the structure is a signature sight to viewers whenever Orioles home games are televised).

tracting AIDS from a blood transfusion he received during back surgery, have shaken but not broken him. Happier days arrived in 2005 when John Fogerty and Fantasy Records (by then a part of the Concord Music Group, a co-owner of which is television luminary Norman Lear), were reunited. This coming together of two old friends resulted in the release by Fantasy Records of "The Long Road Back—The Ultimate John Fogerty-Creedence Collection"—and the launch of "The Long Road Home" world tour. With scheduled stops in Australia, New Zealand, Belgium, Germany, The Netherlands, Denmark, Norway and Sweden as part of this blitz, John Fogerty—one of the one hundred greatest guitarists of all time (as named by Rolling Stone *magazine)—was back!*

> **Only a genuine baseball aficionado could have written and recorded a song like John Fogerty's "Centerfield." That "Centerfield" has found its way onto the public-address systems of ballparks in possibly every state, county, city and town of the country demonstrates that it is arguably second only to "Take Me Out To The Ballgame" in describing the lure the game holds for millions of devotees. Four lines in particular bring goose bumps every time a baseball fan hears them: "Got a beat-up glove, a homemade bat, and brand-new pair of shoes/You know I think it's time to give this game a ride/ Just to hit the ball and touch 'em all—a moment in the sun/(pop) It's gone and you can tell that one goodbye!"**

At least since the 1980s, various doomsayers have predicted that Baseball is dying; a victim, if their pronunciations are to be believed, of the avariciousness of those from whom most followers of the game take their cue: the "fat-cat" owners of professional franchises—and the richly rewarded athletes who work for them. Together, these bloodsuckers at the top are killing the sport, is the claim.

The pundits who voice such assertions (members of the media, sociologists, academics) summon all sorts of "evidence" to buttress their arguments. They cite falling attendance in major-league ballparks; sagging television ratings for the sport; the mediocrity that has arisen from an over-saturation of the market; the rise in popularity of other sports (NASCAR, soccer, women's athletics, golf, etc.); a decided lack of interest on the part of today's kids (as manifested by the disappearance of pick-up games of the sort that used to be so common on sandlots and street corners from San Diego to the Bronx).

In their zeal to call "Strike three!" and send Baseball trudging back to the dugout with its head hanging in shame like "Mighty Casey," the "experts" ignore a simple but powerful truth: Baseball is so intrinsically clean and unblemished that no tomfoolery—not even the machinations of gluttons—can tarnish it beyond repair in the eyes of the public. Not the "Black Sox" Scandal, not Pete Rose, not steroids. The game Abner Doubleday gave a nation endures because of its inherent virginity.

Baseball's eternal attraction is wrapped up in more than a century's worth of sights, sounds and scents. These trappings of history are preserved not only in newspaper clippings, books, photographs, recordings, museum displays and video footage but also in the consciousness of all of those who have been touched by the game's never-ending appeal.

In my own case there is the pride I felt snaring a tennis ball in the web of my Rawlings glove as it caromed back to me from the concrete steps of my childhood home during a "warm-up" session, or seeing my Babe Ruth-league manager point to me as I stood in a circle of boys anxiously awaiting tryouts for the start of the new season and saying, "You're my shortstop."

And there are the following equally-compelling images, which, accrued over the years from personal witness or from other gleanings, now lay stacked like a pile of Adirondack bats at my feet—cementing my allegiance to "The Game" forever; at any moment I can bend over and pick one up and test it for heft and feel just as I used to wrap my

An autographed picture of Babe Ruth on display at a museum near Camden Yards in his boyhood hometown of Baltimore celebrates a song written about his home run-hitting prowess; the image of "Batterin' Babe" along with the sight of a car parked at a rest stop on the New York State Thruway with its destination clearly indicated are testament to the continuing allure of baseball—our National Pastime.

hands around the handle of a thirty two-ounce bat that bore the signature of Nellie Fox, Joe DiMaggio, Henry Aaron, Roberto Clemente or Ted Williams:

- Ernie Banks ("Mr. Cub"), his dimpled cheeks aglow in the afternoon sunshine at Wrigley Field; shouting, as if for all the world to hear, "Let's play two!" (doubleheaders were more common then).

- Stan "The Man" Musial lacing a single into right field for the St. Louis Cardinals ("the Redbirds"), and afterwards, with a towel covering his waist, firing up a cigar in the locker room while talking with the "scribes" about going 3-for-4.

- Dizzy Dean describing a lazy fly ball to the outfield—in working the "Game of the Week" on television with Pee Wee Reese (long before Joe Buck and Tim McCarver came onto the scene)—as "a can of corn" because of the relative ease with which the defender would make the catch.

- Melodious-voiced Mel Allen opening a radio broadcast with the phrase that became his trademark: "Hello again, everybody!"

- A pinstriped Lou Gehrig ("The Iron Horse"), fatally ill with a neuromuscular disease, his voice hoarse, speaking the immortal words "I am the luckiest man on the face of this earth" into a microphone at home plate at Yankee Stadium at a tribute held for him on July 4, 1939. He died at the age of thirty-seven.

- Harry Carey leading fans at the Chicago White Sox's Comiskey Park in a rendition of "Take Me Out to the Ballgame," or funny-man Bob Uecker being told, in the old television commercial, that he was in the wrong section and responding, "Oh, I must be in the good seats!"

- Kevin Costner waxing almost-tearfully poetic about the sport he so adores during his "intro" for TV coverage of the All-Star Game (aka "The Mid-Summer Classic") at Boston's Fenway Park on July 13, 1999.

- Dick Young of the New York Daily News—a working-man's sports-writer, notepad in hand—interviewing Casey Stengel behind the batting cage at the big ball yard in the Bronx (fascinated, I had my binoculars on them the whole time).

- Carleton Fisk literally pushing his high fly ball over the "Green Monster" at Fenway Park from his vantage point along the first-base line in Game 6 of the 1975 World Series.

- Willie Mays' cap flying off as he rounds second, headed for third.

- Sammy Sosa patting his chest in appreciation of fans' applause as he completes his ritualistic sprint to his position in the outfield.

- Kenny Rogers singing "The Greatest," a simple song with a profound message about a little boy, a bat and a ball.

- Ken "The Hawk" Harrelson clubbing a home run over the left-field fence at Johnson Field in Johnson City, New York, for the old Binghamton Triplets, or Dave "King Kong" Kingman "going yard" onto the roof of a bus sitting in the parking lot at Shea Stadium for the New York Mets.

- Usually mild-mannered Jim Leland, manager of the Detroit Tigers, interrupting his pre-game dressing down of an umpire so that both could doff their caps for the National Anthem and then scurrying back in front of the man in blue when the last strains of the music had played to pick up the tirade exactly where he'd left off.

- "No. 7" doffing his hat in gratitude for the cheers and gifts with which he is being showered on "Mickey Mantle Day" (I was watching from the third deck, right over the Yankee dugout, with my dad—just the two of us; it's still my favorite "Baseball moment").

The Atlantic will continue to eat away at the sands of Cape Cod; the right whale will continue to fight for its very survival; forests will continue to give way to housing developments and shopping malls…but so long as there is springtime and a "brown-eyed handsome man" swinging for the fences, there will be Baseball.

IX. TREES

"I'll buy you tall, tall trees
On all the waters and the seas"

"Tall, Tall Trees"
Alan Jackson
Arista Records, 1995

I n many regards Alan Jackson is the atypical Country artist: born into a large blue-collar family in Newnan, Georgia on October 17, 1958, he demonstrated no early pronounced ability in music—or decided inclination toward making the industry his career. It was this very environment, however, that molded the man his fans know today: the son of hardworking parents who married his sweetheart (Denise Jackson), moved to a tiny basement apartment in Nashville, hooked up with Glen Campbell's publishing company, fathered three daughters and went on to write and sing tracks that became hits and in some cases classics. There were the breakthrough smashes of the early 1990s: "I'd Love You All Over Again," "Don't Rock the Jukebox," "Someday," "Midnight in Montgomery," "Love's Got a Hold on You," "She's Got Rhythm (And I Got the Blues)" and "Chattahoochee." And that was just the start. Originals or remakes including "Tall, Tall Trees" and "Itty Bitty" continued his drive to the top. Alan Jackson's intense honesty permeates all of his work; this became most apparent when he unveiled "Where Were You (When the World Stopped Turning)" at the 2001 CMA Awards show; the post-September 11th single raised goose bumps and touched

This park in Worcester would not be nearly as idyllic a scene were it not for a tree situated alongside a parking area at its southern flank. Take the tree away and there are no spring buds seen to sprout, no shade from the summer heat, no golden color to observe in the fall, no branches laden with snow come winter.

hearts. It left his audience stunned—and deeply moved. It won him his first Grammy in 2002. Alan Jackson's emergence as a giant in his field is a tribute not only to his clear, strong voice but his willingness to be candid with his lyrics; indicative of this openness is the song "It's Five O'Clock Somewhere"—a fun drinking-song duet with Jimmy Buffett. Still the same unaffecting person he was as a kid growing up in the Deep South and as a young adult who once labored as a mechanic, a used-car salesman and a forklift operator, he now performs before large crowds in name venues from coast to coast. He has put his talents to good use.

Trees are the fodder for all kinds of things that embellish life: lumber for houses and sheds and cabinets; paper for newsprint; maple syrup; nuts; fruit; leaves for mulch. They also, by their very existence, offer stability.

A climber's appreciation for the simple thing known as a tree is no different than a sparrow's, a hawk's, a heron's, a horticulturist's, a bookworm's, a pilot's, a landscaper's, an urban planner's or an apple grower's. All of the aforementioned recognize the unique place trees occupy in the order of the universe: a position no less vital to "the perpetual balance" than the ones claimed by rivers and streams, lakes and mountains, the sun and moon, clouds, rain and wind, daylight and nighttime.

As a youth, my younger brother Randy spent hours on end in the woods. He scaled the gnarly bark of a maple or a spruce as if he had been endowed with the agility and grasp of a squirrel or a monkey. He swung from limb to limb like Tarzan. He surveyed whole kingdoms from a perch in the branches eighty or a hundred feet off the ground (a pleasure only a few people ever get to enjoy, when you stop and think about it). My mother told me he once tied a ribbon to a tree's upper reaches to let anyone who followed in his footsteps know how high he'd climbed (as if that was likely to occur). He built "tree huts" that afforded him respite from the tumult that constantly grinds and swirls at "base zero." He had no real desire to be caught up in the maelstrom of activity that is found in a pedestrian environment largely populated by Donald Trump and Martha Stewart wannabes.

My own children, when they visited, often pattered after him and his dog "Patches" along a narrow, thorny, muddy trail that began behind my parents' house. They ventured only a short distance before his quickened pace left them struggling to keep up. And then he was gone, disappearing into the denser tangle of thicket as they strained to hear his fading footsteps. They turned toward home, content to wait in the comfort and safety of the living room for his return from "the wild." Back again, his supple arms drenched in perspiration, his light skin reddened by the elements, his shoulder-length hair smelling of pine tar, he would regale his nieces and nephew with stories of his latest escapade.

To them, he was a modern-day Grizzly Adams. They would not have been surprised to see him traipsing toward them with a bear in tow.

My experiences with trees have been tamer in comparison—yet similarly fortifying. No one picks his way steadily higher—feeling for the next strong branch to grab hold of while carefully listening for the telltale cracking sound that would signify a potentially calamitous plunge from the security of "the nest" to injury, or death—a lesser person. The conqueror, having vanquished the beast, is transformed: the sense of accomplishment is so profound that the climber now believes any impasse can be breached, any hurdle cleared, any problem solved.

This explains why, when Anne Morrow Lindbergh—her voice ringing with alarm—rushed to the kitchen table to alert her husband that their young son had begun an ascent of the tree in the yard, Charles Lindbergh did not rise from his seat for a look, or express mutual concern. Lindbergh's own grappling with seemingly impossible situations as an aviator unimpressed by the enormity of the task set before him had spawned a man of fierce determination and independence; this testing had also taught him that nothing shapes a person's will quite so effectively as "trial by fire." Hence his instructions to his wife to "let the boy be."

My encounters with "Tall, Tall Trees" have presented me with a per- spective on the lay of the land that could not have been secured at eye level. Trees' usefulness extends well beyond that role, however. On a platform of boards stitched together between three trees that stand in a closely knit triangle, my boyhood friends and I (with our makeshift bows and arrows at our side) would picture ourselves roaming the countryside, a la Robin Hood and his band of merry men—robbing from the rich to give to the poor (we never got that far, although the idea of it remains tantalizing).

As a teenager, I would rest on my back beneath a giant willow that occupied a prominent place in my folks' side yard; there, in the shade provided by the tree's branches and leaves, which drooped toward the ground like the golden locks of a Greek warrior—forming a natural refuge—I would dream away lazy summer afternoons. Or read comic books.

Now, as an adult, my association with trees is principally limited to uttering exclamations of disbelief at the sight of an oak—having taken root in the flowerbed in the back yard—shoot toward the sky. Jack's beanstalk could not possibly have fired a witness's ardor for any phe- nomenon that borders on the supernatural more than mine is as I watch this oak acquire height inch by inch. At a full forty-five feet, it has attained such size and girth as to suggest the image of a burly sen- tinel in its adapted role—standing guard over the southwest corner of the property, and shading it.

Even one such tree, placed on a street that is otherwise sadly almost bereft of substantial vegetation these days, tends to raise spirits. This is especially true as one tree after another—diseased, or dead—disap- pears from the neighborhood.

This tree, our oak, will eventually succumb to age or infirmity—as all living things do. While among us, however—though mute—it emits an unmistakable bellow.

God is good.

Frank Allen of Kingston, New York had his feet firmly planted in the Atlantic at Nantasket Beach in Hull and was reading a book about the Civil War (and highlighting passages in it) on a perfect beach day in August of 2006 when he agreed to pose for a picture. He has been frequenting Nantasket for many years. For a moment in time, as they discussed vocations and vacations, total strangers were united by a mutual fondness for sand, sun and surf.

X. Beaches

"We'll all be planning out
a route we're gonna take real soon.
We're waxing down our surfboards,
we can't wait for June.
We'll all be gone for the summer.
We're on safari to stay.
Tell the teacher we're surfin'.
Surfin' U.S.A."

"Surfin' U.S.A."
The Beach Boys
Capitol Records, 1962

I t is not enough to say that The Beach Boys produce a "sound" that is uniquely theirs. While their ability to harmonize like no other Rock & Roll band before or after (with the possible exception of The Eagles) is justifiably championed (they were at one time more popular among Britons, as a vocal group, than The Beatles, and at the height or their prowess they reeled off twenty albums over a seven-year period, in the 1960s), their greatness transcends that distinction. To me, they define what it means to be a Californian, in a state, as an article in The New Yorker magazine once put it, where "the light" is more pure and intense than perhaps anywhere else on earth. That so many of their songs, starting with "Surfin'," in 1961, and including "Fun, Fun, Fun," "Good Vibrations," "California Girls" and of course the later smash hit "Kokomo" (my personal favorite) conjure up images of a lifestyle in which leisure trumps labor only strengthens the identity they have created for themselves. That they have withstood a number of blows (the often-intrusive influence of the Wilson brothers' father, Murry

Wilson, the drowning death of Dennis Wilson in 1983, the passing of Carl Wilson in 1998) to remain one of the world's premier live acts is a tribute to the talents of Brian Wilson, first cousin Mike Love, Al Jardine and the other members of the band. When I am bound for the beach, The Beach Boys go with me; I would have it no other way.

The closest I have come to "riding the big one" is skimming across the surface of the ocean on a boogie board in the chill waters of the Atlantic in Massachusetts, Rhode Island and New Hampshire. While the charge this amusement affords amounts to only a fraction of the rush surfers get from their own singular pursuit, I can identify with their love of the water as it is described so well in "Surfin' U.S.A." by The Beach Boys:
"If ev'rybody had an ocean across the U.S.A.
Then ev'rybody'd be surfin', like Califor-I-A
You'd see 'em wearing their baggies, Huariachi sandals too
A bushy bushy blonde hairdo, Surfin' U.S.A."

It is not surprising that when people ponder rejuvenation, their thoughts quite naturally turn to "the beach." The very mention of the words triggers images that provide spontaneous warmth: logs on the fire, soup on the stove, blankets on the bed, sweaters in the dresser drawer.

Growing up hundreds of miles from the ocean, my association with beaches did not fully materialize until a new job brought our family to Massachusetts in 1985. To be deposited at the epicenter of the American Revolution at the age of forty—with such reminders of the events that helped forge a nation as Concord and Lexington, Old North Church, the Freedom Trail, Boston Harbor, the U.S.S. Constitution, Dorchester Heights and Bunker Hill close by—is cause enough to savor the splen-diferous fortunes that can fall into one's lap when they are least expected. To land as well not much farther than a wave length from beaches that are so alluring and so pristine that they could only have been sculpted by the hand of the Almighty is a bonus of colossal magnitude: literally the pot of gold at the end of the rainbow.

They beckon from the north, south and east (leaving the west to those who prefer lakes and mountains), whispering in my ear: "Come; taste; enjoy."

Their assets—equally compelling, but individually exclusive—deepen the dilemma that inevitably arises when a choice must be made.

There is Salisbury, where it is not unusual to spot horses afoot (the fried dough is to die for too); Plymouth, where large rocks protrude from the water like monuments (some are draped in red, white and blue); Narragansett, where the likelihood of encountering tolerable water temperatures is good; Misquanmicut, where the surf churns and tumbles: a maelstrom that entices the adventurous to wade in at their own peril; Newport, where the coziness of the cove-like setting is embellished by the sight of skimpily clad babes swatting a volleyball back and forth to the drumbeat of Led Zeppelin and AC/DC; Ogunquit, Wells and Old Orchard, where the shorelines are largely uncorrupted by the tentacles of progress; Gloucester, where the attraction is partly the spectacle of surfers (almost always in wet suits) gathering themselves, one by one and in groups of two and three—Riders of the Storm—to undertake another run at immortality; Galilee, where the added thrill of watching the ferry boat load and leave for Block Island, or purchasing an order of French fries from George's, awaits;Revere and Wollaston, which rock around the clock in the very shadow of the city; Point Judith, where there is lots of room to stretch and play; and Nauset and Marconi and Newcomb Hollow, where the chance to experience first-hand the enthrallments Patti Page famously chronicled in the song "Old Cape Cod" are ever-present.

These constitute a sampling of goodies more inviting than a box of Whitman's chocolates.

And then there is the strip of sand in Hull, Massachusetts known as Nantasket, hard against the Atlantic and with Boston's skyline magnificently visible from the town's northernmost tip (aptly named "World's End").

Even with only a smattering of remnants left from its heyday as a summertime playground, when Paragon Park (an amusement-lover's paradise) drew throngs from all corners of the East Coast, Nantasket remains a beach town that is always a treat. It can claim, as perhaps no other community is able to, ocean views from virtually every upper-story window and second or third-floor deck. The sights are even more spectacular from the multi-million dollar homes occupying spits of land along Ocean Drive as the road winds and turns south toward Cohasset and from smaller residences at sea level within the "Alphabet" streets or from the palatial homes that are sprinkled across Allerton Hill.

The dismantling of Paragon Park's roller coaster (the most conspicuous symbol of Nantasket's onetime irresistible charm) generated anguished headlines in newspapers throughout Massachusetts (and the appropriate gnashing of teeth to accompany them). The crowds fell off as a result of this calamity; and yet on a warm day, irrespective of the season, but particularly during July and August, the sidewalks of Hull Shore Drive, and the beach itself, directly below, teem with a cross-section of humanity: roller bladers, motorcyclists (most made it a habit to gather across the street from the biker-bar "The Dry Dock," before it was seized for back taxes), joggers, skateboarders, power walkers, gold diggers, bodybuilders, lovers, mothers pushing baby carriages, fathers hoisting toddlers onto their shoulders for a quick dip, lifeguards swimming in a pack like dolphins from north to south as part of a training regimen, food seekers (patronizing the Trolley Dog, now operating under a different name, and The Red Parrot with its deck-dining appeal), kite flyers, sun worshippers and of course the always-conspicuous locals in their visor caps and sneakers—reluctantly but not disagreeably sharing their "private" domain with the invaders who rush in for a piece of the action.

The planes of Logan drone overhead, as if their pilots cannot subdue the urge to show off the jewel that shimmers thousands of feet below.

For the frequent visitor, Nantasket never fails to enthrall; this is true even when the tide is in, devouring more and more of the beach until at last it is lapping at the floodwall and there is no recourse but to pack up the gear and retreat to dry ground.

In seeming recognition of its singular appeal, Nantasket strains to outshine its previous most dazzling effort. And it succeeds. Unforgettable moments "at Nantasket" multiply with each fresh encounter. My own are neither few nor insignificant. High on the list is meeting and bagging the autograph of Phil Everly of The Everly Brothers at the new Clarion Nantasket Beach Hotel on Hull Shore Drive a few summers ago.

We had taken in The Everly Brothers' show at the South Shore Music Circus the evening before; over breakfast, after being informed by our waitress that we'd missed the best part of all ("the boys came back here and jammed in the lounge for a while," she said), I could not contain my chagrin at having retired for the night too soon. At that instant Phil Everly walked into the dining room, alone, and took a seat at a table. I did not hesitate long enough to contemplate the possibility of rejection; I strode toward him, introduced myself, offered my compliments on the performance, and thrust a piece of paper at him. He cordially obliged with an autograph. My ship, as Bob Dylan has said, had come in.

I have stretched out on the sand at Virginia Beach, walked the edges of the ocean at Siesta Key in Sarasota and at Daytona Beach, strode the boardwalk at Atlantic City, dodged the jellyfish at Rehoboth Beach. Where water meets sand is a place so serene and so invigorating that it is constantly calling me with these words: "come back to the beach."

There are people who walk, and then there is Thomas Castonguay. Otherwise known as "TomCat," he can be seen ambling along the sidewalks of Worcester at different hours of the day—in attire perfectly suited for the purpose. I ran into him for the first (and only time, so far) on a fine October afternoon, and was taken with his "get-up:" wide-brimmed hat (peppered with "campaign" buttons), hooded garment, jeans, sneakers and walking stick. Comfortable hoofing to and fro in the heart of the city, "TomCat" would be just as "at home" on a dusty country road!

XI. WALKING

"I'm walkin' to New Orleans
I've got no time for talkin'
I've got to keep on walkin'
New Orleans is my home"

"Walking to New Orleans"
Fats Domino
Imperial Records, 1960

My heart broke a little when the news flashed on the radio that the whereabouts of "The Fat Man" were not known in the immediate aftermath of the flooding in New Orleans caused by Hurricane Katrina. In the days that followed, as Fats Domino fans in every corner of the globe waited to hear whether he was alive or dead, Doo Wop Deejay Milton Cordeiro of WCUW in Worcester (91.3 FM) played "Walking to New Orleans" as a tribute to "The Fat Man." For reasons that remain a mystery, I had never heard the song before, and instantly liked it; which is not surprising since there is little in Fats Domino's repertoire that I find less than terrific. When listening to his "Greatest Hits" album, I often end up singing along (woefully, I must admit) to "Hello Josephine" ("Hello, Josephine/How do you do?/Do you remember me baby/like I remember you?"), "Blueberry Hill," "Let The Four Winds Blow," "I'm Ready," "Whole Lotta Lovin' " or "Ain't That A Shame." Born in New Orleans on February 28, 1928, Antoine "Fats" Domino learned to play the piano at the age of seven and released his first record, "The Fat Man"—an on-the-spot hit—in 1949. "The Fat Man" is

considered in some circles to be the first Rock & Roll song ever recorded. Fats'
collaborations with bandleader/songwriter/trumpeter Dave Bartholomew
resulted in a string of R&B and Top 100-smash records. Fats also performed
in four Rock & Roll movies. The very face of New Orleans Rhythm & Blues,
he went on to become a crossover sensation with thirty-five Top 40 Pop sin-
gles between 1955 and 1963. It was a relief to learn that he had survived
Katrina and that the infectious smile for which "The Fat Man" is famous
would remain intact for a while longer.

**The longest walk I ever took was actually a twenty
two-mile forced march, part of tying together the final
stages of basic training our platoon was involved in at
the U.S. Marine Corps facility at Parris Island, South
Carolina. As we trudged ahead under the weight of a
full complement of gear—and with blazing summer
heat turning shin splints in our legs into daggers—my
buddy Dennis Mottola kept glancing to the side.
There, the unit's despised lead drill instructor, Sgt.
Cox—seemingly unfettered by the ordeal—was calling
cadence from beneath his wide-brimmed hat. Picking
up the chant, Mottola altered the words. "Will not
stop, till Cox drops," he said. Somehow, we made it.**

It is a well-known fact within my family that I love to walk. Less
apparent to those aware of this compulsion are my reasons for doing
so. Not that there has been a conscientious effort on my part to keep
my motivations a secret; I am different in that regard, then, than my
friends George and Marion Busada of Worcester, who share the ingredients of the sauce that tops their legendary "Speedy burger" with no
one.

I must say that the Busadas demonstrate the wisdom of lords and
kings in keeping their magic formula shrouded in darkness; the con-
cealment only heightens the mystery surrounding the concoction—

thus intensifying its appeal all the more (as "classified information" is wont to do). Not even members of the cruising crowd who patronized the Busadas' drive-in restaurant when it was still operating know "the mix." Over time these young people acquired the status of sons and daughters by virtue of the bond that developed between them and the Busadas during "the Speedy years;" they might have then been able to tell you George's date of birth and Marion's favorite meal. But "The Recipe?" Not a chance.

I would not be so presumptuous as to suggest that my yen for walking has produced jaunts equal in magnitude to the ones undertaken by Henry David Thoreau. Thoreau's forays into the fields and woodlands in and around Concord effectively established his reputation as a rambler of renown. Nor were his expeditions (always accompanied by a journal and a pencil, and sometimes by his companion the poet William Ellery Channing Jr.) limited to his home turf; his several visits to Cape Cod, which occurred over a span of about six years, starting in 1849 and ending in 1855, produced walks, as he put it, "from Eastham to Provincetown twice on the Atlantic side, and once on the Bay side also, excepting four or five miles…" He also "crossed the Cape," he said, "half a dozen times" (Thoreau's famous conclusion after his inspections of its mid-to-lower extremities were done, by the way, was that "the Cape" had a singular allure as an outpost; "A man may stand there and put all America behind him," he said).

By his own figuring, Thoreau's total association with Cape Cod amounted to no more than three weeks. Yet it spawned the book Cape Cod (first published in the United States in 1865). Cape Cod—despite the criticism it provoked among reviewers for being too this or too that—boils to an essence Thoreau's sobering contemplations on the shipwrecked corpses, flotsam, craggy cliffs and dunes, ponds, swamps, "Nauset women," oystermen, seals, blackfish (beached pilot whales), bank swallows, crows, crabs, harbors, lodges, taverns and lighthouses he encountered as he explored a then mostly-untamed and yet captivatingly beautiful place.

Thoreau's sauntering amid the quiet sands of this initially remote and largely uncivilized "elbow" of Massachusetts compelled Adam Gamble, a former newspaper reporter, to publish *In the Footsteps of Thoreau/25 Historic & Nature Walks on Cape Cod*, in 1997. *In the Footsteps* pays due homage to Thoreau's proverbial wanderlust; it goes beyond that, however, to recreate for the pleasure of "Thoreauvians" everywhere "hikes" ranging in difficulty from easy to severe in order that they may, as Gamble has, discover "the many wonders of Cape Cod for themselves." Hence a description of the walk along the Yarmouth Historical Society Trails: distance, 1.5 miles; time, forty-five minutes—a non-strenuous pilgrimage. Or, in sharp contrast, from Marconi Beach to LeCount Hollow Beach: distance, 8.1 miles; time, five hours—an extremely taxing adventure.

Like Thoreau, Peter Jenkins, author of the breakthrough *A Walk Across America*—and a number of subsequent works about the pastime of walking that have established him as an expert on the subject—hungered to strike out for territories foreign to his eyes for the express purpose of bringing new meaning to his life. Thoreau said it in these words: "My desire for knowledge is intermittent, but my desire to bathe my head in atmospheres unknown to my feet is perennial and constant." Jenkins' urge was similar; he said, "I started out searching for myself and my country, and found both."

Disillusioned with society in the 1970s, Jenkins and his trusty dog Cooper saddled up and struck forth—uncertain of what the next kilometer, the next hill or the next morning would bring. Like Thoreau, the fresh air Jenkins drew through his nostrils in huge drafts as he stalked the land with boots laced and knapsack slung from his shoulders changed his perspective forever. The scenes he witnessed, the situations he experienced and the people he met (mountain men, small-town bullies, ranchers, farmers, seminary students, sawmill workers, religious cult leaders) transformed him.

So it is no closely guarded reason, why I walk, and why I do so at every opportunity and with little concern for where the spirit of the moment may lead me or for how long it will take. I stride the sidewalks of Linwood, the paths of the Blackstone Canal, the streets of Rehoboth Beach (on our annual excursions there to see Soren and Norma Nielsen—dear members of the family, both), and other environments, for the oxygen that fills my lungs, the blessed warmth the sun delivers to my cheeks and back and the purging of cares and worries the exercise brings to my head. When I walk I can dream and plan. I can think.

Once in Worcester there was a man affectionately known as "The Whistler;" I used to spot him in the Vernon Hill area. Clad in Bermuda shorts, sneakers and a tank top and tanned from head to toe, he was a local celebrity whose fast-paced walking was punctuated by a throaty high-pitched and deliriously melodious whistle that carried far across the landscape and lingered in the air. People would honk the horns of their cars in recognition of sighting him, and in the expectation that a whistle—rendered in reciprocation—would follow. And it always did; accompanied by a cheerful wave of one hand or the other. The robins, sparrows, chickadees, blue jays and finches must have been jealous as they sat by and listened to the cacophony of sound that was being created around them; they must have wondered where on earth such a species of music maker could have come from, who could fill the neighborhood with wondrous notes.

The birds certainly must have concluded, as I did, that "The Whistler" was a deliriously contented man; and that his joy was directly related to the activity that occupied his attention at that particular moment: walking!

My earth angel, the former Doris Marie Joiner, left, first appeared to me on Christmas Night 1967: not in a dream but on a blind date. I have pinched myself repeatedly since as assurance that she is in fact real and not a figment of my imagination. Together now for thirty-eight years (as of early '07), we are not two but one: linked in the conviction that the union created by an exchange of vows in a Methodist church in Vestal, New York on a sultry September day was, as Woody Guthrie would say, "bound for glory." Moment by moment, mile by mile from the instant the train left the station, she has been by my side; together we have traveled the tracks where they have led, certain in our minds—and our hearts—that we were meant to take the journey hand-in-hand. Pictured with us in this photograph is Marie's sister Sarah; once, we were all young!

XII. True love

"Hey, hey, good lookin',
Watcha got cookin'?
How's about cookin' somethin'
up with me?
Hey, sweet baby,
Don't you think maybe
we could find us
A brand new recipe?"

"Hey, Good Lookin' "
Hank Williams
MGM Records, 1951

C all him Hiriam, which is his given name, call him "Luke the Drifter," which is the "transparent pseudonym" he developed for himself, call him "the father of Contemporary Country Music," which is how he is appropriately known in Nashville, or just call him "the late great Hank Williams." However he is identified, Hank Williams looms large in the annals of American music. With little more musical training than the learning he picked up as a youngster in Georginia, Alabama, from a black street musician, Rufus Payne, a.k.a. "Tee-Tot," and with the handicap of ill health hanging over him like a dark cloud every step of the way, Hank Williams managed to leave a well-marked trail for other aspiring artists to follow. Many are indebted to him for the standard he set with his songwriting and singing abilities. Although his life was short and tragic, it stands as an example of the soaring achievement that is possible when the will refuses to accept mediocrity. There was in Hank Williams the self-confidence that produced such *early gems as "Move It On Over" and "Honky Tonkin.' " There was also the conviction that a song like "Lovesick Blues" was worth the effort; over the strenuous objections of those who predicted it didn't have a chance, Hank Williams got it released in February of 1949. "Lovesick Blues" was an instant success. It gave his career a kick-start; appearances with his band "The Drifting Cowboys" at beer joints and regional shows and stints on KWKH/Shreveport's Saturday-night jamboree "the Louisiana Hayride" were replaced by invitations to the Opry. Before long, and with the help of Fred Rose of Acuff-Rose, who believed in him, Hank Williams was Country's brightest talent. He remains an inspiring influence.*

There is love, and then there is a love that knows no equal. The difference between the two is profound.

Men can argue unto Eternity if any such phenomenon as "love at first sight" exists; some among us, nevertheless, are able to assert with a degree of certitude that the heart is indeed smitten upon meeting "the right one"—whether at the start of the trip, or farther down the road. It doesn't matter how late in life the rendezvous of souls who are "destined" to be together occurs; because, whether the ensuing relationship lasts for a day—or decades—it will have been worth the wait.

It was my own good fortune for such an encounter to have taken place many years ago, on a blind date—on Christmas Night, 1967 (which raises the question: Was God, Santa Claus, Lady Luck, or all three, responsible?). The union that was forged from that meeting has withstood virtually every test Fate can conceive: philosophical disagreements; financial impediments; emotional fluctuations; personal reversals; even individual tastes that are not always completely in sync (she likes Country, my first choice is Rock…she is always in search of flowers and swans, I prefer car shows…she watches the Cooking channel, I favor the Golf channel; etc.).

It comes back to the engrossed, beseeching look she leveled on me with those mesmerizing hazel eyes in our initial moments alone—and to the affection that developed between us in the days and weeks of courtship that followed. Ours was a fast-paced and torrid romance that erupted like Vesuvius after we had finished working the three-to-eleven shift, and mostly on the sofa in her parents' living room as The Platters or Johnny Mathis or Andy Williams rendered vocal accompaniment but also in the front and back seat of her Volkswagen. We were two people ravenous for an alliance of the sort that neither of us had yet experienced; the heavens, in turn, responded affirmatively. At first, it was the physical pull we were both feeling that drew me to her. Soon, it was something far more compelling, as I became aware of traits so deeply ingrained in her that no force can shake them loose: honesty; loyalty; integrity; generosity; unerringly sound judgment.

She is the better of the two of us in ways that only she and I appear to understand, as she continues to fret over the health and well-being of the three darlings we brought into the world, as she metes out swift and sure discipline to a grandchild who is misbehaving, as she heads back to the supermarket to tell the cashier that he inadvertently undercharged her by a dollar and fifty-three cents, as she reminds me not to leave matches lying on the dining-room table, as she nudges me to stop gawking and daydreaming and to pay attention instead to exit signs on the highway, as she writes notes to herself so that she will not forget all of the things she needs to take care of, as she reaches for me in the darkness of the night and attends to my every need, as she looks at life with the seriousness of a country preacher while I laugh myself silly at the inanity of it all.

Together, we make it work. Still, there is no question in my mind as to which of us brings the most to the collaboration. She is lead oarsman and the one who can be depended on to always pull in the right direction.

Now, after all this time has passed, I ask myself: how could I have been so blessed...to have such a wise and true best friend as this?

The look offered by our beloved Sheba was one of total allegiance, as is so typical of the species. Partly lame from the time we took her in, she never uttered so much as a whimper of protest at being less than perfect—physically. She was the very definition of decency and goodness.

XIII. Dogs

"Johnny is a joker that's
a'tryin' to steal my baby
(he's a bird dog)
Hey, bird dog get away from my quail
Hey, bird dog you're on the wrong trail"

"Bird Dog"
The Everly Brothers
Cadence Records, 1958

Amid the stack of 45 RPM records I owned as a fourteen and fifteen-year-old were several featuring The Everly Brothers. It was an amazing thing, two hillbilly singers from Western Kentucky having the kind of influence they did on kids my age growing up in faraway upstate New York. Yet Don and Phil Everly spoke to me in a profoundly personal way with songs that captured all of the tumultuousness and heartache of teenage romance. I was twelve and beginning to feel the surges of desire when "Bye Bye Love" was released in 1957; the opening words of that track (it reached No. 2 on the Pop charts and remained in that lofty sphere for twenty-seven weeks) were a portent of the agony to come: "Bye bye, love. Bye bye, happiness. Hello, loneliness. I think I'm a-gonna cry..." Between 1957 and 1962, The Everly Brothers turned the budding medium known as Rock & Roll on its head. Their beautiful two-part harmonies stood in stark contrast to the raucousness of such early Rockers as Jerry Lee Lewis, Little Richard and Chuck Berry, and earned them instant fame with the Cadence label and a huge, avid following. Furthermore, with their lyrics they literally walked

their way into the bedrooms of boys and girls not much younger than them-
selves by putting into song the roller-coaster emotions we were feeling about
puppy love, parents, teachers and "outsiders" (especially adults) who just
didn't understand. The singles that followed "Bye Bye Love" tugged every bit
as strongly: "All I Have to Do Is Dream," "Take a Message to Mary," "('Til)
I Kissed You" and "Let It Be Me." And then came their biggest hit ever:
"Cathy's Clown," recorded with Warner Brothers, which reinforced their hold
on America's youth. With the lines "Don't want your lo-o-o-o-ove anymore/I
die each time I hear this sound:/Don't want your kisses, that's for sure/Here
he co-o-o-o-omes. That's Cathy's Clown," The Everly Brothers once again
struck a note that resonated with American youth who were experiencing the
thrills and chills of the adolescent dating scene. By 1973, however—beset by
personal problems and with their luster overshadowed by The Beatles—The
Everly Brothers suffered a breakup of their own. Their last performance
together, at Knotts Berry Farm in California, was a debacle; Phil, furious
with Don's drunken behavior, stormed off the stage halfway through the
show. Except at their father Ike's funeral in 1975, they did not speak again
for ten years. The estrangement made their reuniting, in a celebrated con-
cert at Royal Albert Hall in London in 1983, that much more exhilarating
for The Everly Brothers and their millions of devotees around the globe. The
brief comments Phil Everly made on that occasion were all that needed to be
said: "It's good to be back!"

> **Even taking into account the dogs I've run into that did**
> **not welcome my presence, starting with "King," whose**
> **main objective in life must have been to rise out of a lazy**
> **slumber and bare his fangs at me when I tried to deliver**
> **the newspaper to his owners' residence as a boy, I have**
> **always considered dogs a gift. On balance they rank high**
> **on God's list of "all creatures great and small."**

Somewhere on a hill in upstate New York lie the bones of "Queenie,"
the first dog I knew. A collie, she followed me to school one day (in the

fashion of Mary's little lamb), was struck a glancing blow by the town drunk in his pickup truck, hobbled away, whimpering, and did not return home that evening. My father broke the news that he had buried her, revealing in a voice heavy with sadness that the injuries she had suffered left him no choice but to put her down.

I have always felt that of all the animals man can adopt as pets, dogs are an infinitely better pick than rabbits, hamsters, snakes, parrots, pigs, goats, goldfish, iguanas or any of the rest. They are certainly preferable to cats. Cats rub me the wrong way—literally and figuratively. Their penchant for mischievousness, combined with a personality that is generally aloof save for those moments when they want to be fed, or let out the door, renders them no more interesting than the neighbor whose greeting, day after day, year after year, is confined to a nod of the head (I have had the misfortune to meet a few of those kinds, too).

We once offered temporary refuge to a cat whose primary preoccupation was climbing the walls. I called her "The Calico Cyclone." During the mercifully brief period she spent under our roof, I saw firsthand how enormous a task domestication can be for people like me who in a fit of weakness allow a veritable beast to take up residence; without warning, she would dart across the floor and scramble in a seeming terror-stricken panic up the curtains and leap from there to the kitchen counter. I saw so little of her that she was not much more than a blur. There was nothing wrong with her talons when it came to ripping apart sofas and chairs and lace; her mind was another matter. It may have been mad cow disease for all I know.

Unquestionably, my fondness for dogs stems in large degree from the affinity for them that developed when I was young; this lure was significantly influenced, in turn, by a weekly dose of the television show "Lassie," in which a dog—a collie—performed feats that were every bit as spectacular as those manufactured by Tarzan, The Lone Ranger, Mighty Mouse, Zorro, Superman, Roy Rogers, Gene Autry, Audie Murphy, John Wayne and James Bond.

I came to believe, in watching the escapades of "Lassie," and those of "Rin Tin Tin" (a German Shepherd, and a similarly rescue-oriented animal) that dogs were, by instinct, courageous and loyal creatures; perfectly willing, with no regard for their own survival, to rush forward and drag their master (or any person in distress) from a burning building, to gallop off in a bid to summon help or, if abducted, to escape and find their way back home—no matter how daunting the distance, or how treacherous the terrain.

These days, "Lassie" has been relegated to reruns; my view of dogs' natural-born worthiness as a species remains intact, nevertheless. The two dogs that have shared our domain with us over the years— "Sheba," then "Bogey" (both, regrettably, long gone)—have reinforced my conviction that dogs offer companionship that is so undiluted by external interferences as to be utterly and irrevocably beyond compare.

Even given their particular oddities, our dogs enlivened the household. "Sheba" (a collie/Samoyed mix, with the thick white coat that is a marking of the latter) was saddled with a hip deformity, real or acquired, that caused her to walk kind of sideways. "Bogey" (a Lhasa Apso mix) was beset with a generally disagreeable disposition that prompted our son to jokingly dub him "Bogus."

Nevertheless, neither brought dishonor to their respective breeds. Sheba's status as the family's personal favorite of the two stemmed from a geniality that remained intact even after age and ills reduced her to a helpless heap on the floor in a corner of the dining room. In her prime she was agile enough to jump gracefully from the ground and snatch a Frisbee out of the air with the fluidity of an Olympian and to "wrestle" her master with just the right amount of pretended viciousness typifying her effort. During a portion of the several months I commuted between New York and Massachusetts on a motorcycle after taking a new job, her ears would perk up at the sound of the engine trumpeting my arrival home on Friday nights even though I was still half a street away; at that instant, she would start barking and racing back and forth in breathless anticipation of my appearance.

It was Bogey's destiny to be the victim of two savage attacks by bigger dogs while out for a walk, and the fate of my wife and I to witness both assaults. The first of these took place near the railroad tracks just beyond the state highway a block or so from our house, when a predator came at us in a sudden hell-bent rush and pounced on Bogey with the fury of a tiger. Thankfully, the onslaught lasted only a few seconds and produced no discernible serious injuries.

Bogey had no sooner recovered from that mauling than he was ambushed yet again, this time on a quiet side street not far from a church that sits about three quarters of a mile from our house. As before, he was leashed (proving that law-abiding dogs, like law-abiding citizens, do not always benefit from the adherence they show to rules established by government). The aggressor in this case came roaring at Bogey from its owner's back yard, leaving the human observers of his fury just enough time to watch the charge materialize but not enough to prevent it. He proceeded to sink his teeth into Bogey and to shake him around like a rag doll while three fully grown adults (the two of us and a good-Samaritan female bystander, who entered the fray with a broom in hand) tried for what seemed like an eternity to get him to back off by beating and flailing away in protest. When the thrashing finally ended we were left with a limp and broken pet. We carried him home in our arms. Bogey recovered; considerably the wiser, I subsequently "walked" him only a short distance in any direction, lest he fall prey to a third and potentially even more crippling beating.

For some reason man frequently considers it his solemn duty to return the unequivocal affection dogs demonstrate toward him with treatment usually reserved for rats or ants. I heard it said once that if a man and a dog approached St. Peter's Gate at the same time, God would let the dog—but not the man—in. This is not so hard to believe, given the way man has been known to reward a dog's loyalty with curses, complaints and whippings.

In unforgettably capturing the unwarranted brutality to which a good canine is often subjected, Jack London's *The Call of the Wild* puts

"Buck" in the camp of mean and malicious sled-dog operators like "Perreault" and "Francois" and "Hal," who club and lash their worker animals into a state of compliance. It is not enough that poor Buck must fight to the finish on an almost daily basis with fellow "team" dogs that harbor a jealousy or resentfulness toward him; he must also put up with the blows administered by cruel owners. Not until a man named John Thornton comes along to purchase him does Buck escape from bondage and a certain trip to the grave.

Twice in return for John Thornton's kindly ways, Buck—rejuvenated—saves his new master's life. First, Buck jumps at the throat of a nasty character named "Black" Burton when Burton suddenly strikes out at Thornton after Thornton innocently tries to serve as peacemaker during an altercation at a bar. Another time, when Thornton is pitched from a boat into the raging rapids of "Forty Mile Creek," Buck springs into action in defiance of all odds and successfully drags him to shore.

In a third display of strength that leaves a crowd of several hundred onlookers breathless, Buck, on Thornton's command, pulls a sled laden with twenty fifty-pound sacks of flour a distance of one hundred yards. The feat settles a bet of one thousand dollars in gold dust. The scene leading up to the Buck's grand display of muscle is nothing short of mesmerizing: Buck catching "the contagion of the excitement" as he is harnessed to the sled and sensing that he "must do a great thing for John Thornton," Thornton kneeling at Buck's side and whispering in Buck's ear the words: "As you love me, Buck. As you love me." Then, in quick succession from John Thornton: "Now, Buck," "Gee!" "Haw!" and, finally, "Mush!"

It is a virtuoso performance from start to finish. The legend of Buck as the greatest Alaskan sled dog of them all is firmly cemented.

That it ends badly does not diminish the veracity or the poignancy of the tale Jack London has woven. As an ever-intensifying primordial urge increasingly pulls Buck away from camp to a life spent deep in the forest, where he is able to rendezvous with a wolf "brother" or to bring down a calf, a deer or a moose, his ears and nose suddenly sense calamity. Backtracking in a rush, he finds the bodies of dogs and men, filled with arrows, strewn along the path. They are victims of a band of Yeehat Indians. John Thornton is among the dead. The scene sends Buck into a rage, and he becomes a "fiend incarnate" as he seeks retribution on the perpetrators of the crime. The Yeehats fly into the woods. Their hearts thump at the very thought of so intrepid a stalker racing after them with a rapid and unrelenting vengeance. Never again do they want to come face to face with this blazing force, this "Evil Spirit."

With the murder of John Thornton by ambushers, Buck's last tie to "civilization" is broken. Now, when Buck hears yelps and howls pierce the night air, he knows it is the brethren issuing a clear summons to him. He knows his place is with them.

Not every dog falls into the same class as Buck. The dogs I have encountered, however, are by and large animals whose primary motivation is to be their owner's best friend. This has been the case whether they are small enough to stuff into a coat pocket or too big to lay at one's feet in bed; whether they have straight tails or tails that curl; whether they yelp a lot or a little; whether they are fat or slim; whether they are long-legged or short-legged; whether they like to be petted or are standoffish; whether they are kept inside or allowed to occupy the out of doors; whether they are playful or disinterested in games.

Man could search to the ends of the earth and never find a companion whose faithfulness to him is any more deep and abiding than that exhibited by a dog. Any man who demonstrates less than a full appreciation of this trait is no friend of mine.

Ray Dunphe of Oxford, shown holding a sign in front of Oxford High School for ultimately unsuccessful political candidate Dave Singer in September of 2006, is entirely comfortable with the role—just as he is, costumed, in waving to potential customers of The Coffee Hop, a little ways up the road.

XIV. Politics

"We live in a political world
Turning and a'thrashing about,
As soon as you're awake,
You're trained to take
What looks like the easy way out"

"Political World"
Bob Dylan
Columbia Records, 1989

F ew people truly understand my fascination with Robert Allen
Zimmerman: Bob Dylan. My brother Randy, my son Dan and my
daughter Mandy and her husband Dave are among the handful of people
who "get it." Their appreciation for what this cherub-faced child of the cold
and distant Midwest has accomplished in his chosen profession after striking
out from Hibbing, Minnesota with not much more than pocket change as
fare, a guitar on his back and a dream in his head on his way to New York
City and a rendezvous with his idol—a dying Woody Guthrie—compares
favorably to my own. From his debut as a folk singer in Greenwich Village
coffee houses to the music review by Bob Shelton of The New York Times
that sent him on his way, to his legendary protest songs to his abrupt transformation into a Rock star to his shocking "going electric" at Newport to a
motorcycle accident that almost killed him and that sent him into seclusion,
to his dabbling with Christianity, to the lyrics he has penned for television
shows and movies to the never-ending tour of the world's concert stages in
which he seems to be constantly engaged to the writing of his autobiography

99

Chronicles *and on and on, Bob Dylan has "spoken" to the masses like no one in the history of music: American or otherwise. Some have listened closely as the hundreds upon hundreds of songs have rolled forth: "It Ain't Me, Babe;" "Like A Rolling Stone;" "Subterranean Homesick Blues;" "Hurricane;" "Knockin' On Heaven's Door;" "It's All Over Now, Baby Blue." Some haven't paid any attention. It doesn't matter. What Bob Dylan is saying will continue to resound through the ages, beckoning us to stretch and reach and demand the best of ourselves; to strive for excellence, which is the real message of the vast body of work he has generated to date. No one triggers my creativity like Bob Dylan. Thanks, Bob!*

If love makes the world go round, politics gives it shape. As a student of politics, I am enthralled by its varied appearances—even as I despair over the occasional excesses and infringements it imposes on the daily equilibrium.

How a Protestant who just happens to also be a conservative Republican (most of the time) winds up in a state that is populated by enough native Catholics and liberal Democrats to sink a battleship amounts to a mystery of unfathomable magnitude. It is certainly beyond my capacity to unravel. I would be more easily pressed to explain the evolution of the chrysanthemum than to spell out what it was exactly that lured me to Massachusetts in the spring of 1985 to live and work.

I shudder now to think about having landed, newspaper-career wise, right smack dab at the epicenter of Liberalism—in Brookline, the birthplace of John F. Kennedy and the home of Michael S. Dukakis; a place that is literally crawling with people whose ardency for positions espoused by "The Left" is every bit as intense as that evoked by Barbara Streisand, Alec Baldwin or Martin Sheen.

That I have survived on the very soil from which such titans of the Democratic Party as Ted Kennedy, John Kerry, Marty Meehan, Barney

Frank, Richard Neal and Edward Markey rose to prominence as fire-breathing dragons for their side is no small accomplishment. I can thank ideological compatriots like Harry Berkowitz (the "Mayor of Rockdale," here in Northbridge, and a longtime Massachusetts Republican Party stalwart) and State Rep. George Peterson (a Republican from Grafton who has craftily managed to articulate views that resonate with the citizenry, regardless of the way these individuals typically vote in national elections—and thus to consistently retain his 9th Worcester District seat as a member of a decided minority on Beacon Hill) for the efforts they and others of a similar persuasion have mounted in helping protect my flank from the constant salvoes the amply fortified and heavily prevalent occupying armies propel in my direction.

The truth is, my sentiments have not always rested in the camp defended by spokespersons for "The Right." Nor can it be said that I repeatedly, without exception, support stances taken by the Republican Party today. On the call for reinstitution of the death penalty here in the Commonwealth by then-Gov. Mitt Romney, for instance, I am reluctantly opposed. I agree in principle on the need for administering to the perpetrators of heinous crimes the most stringent punishment the law will allow; the rub comes in the misgivings I harbor about government's ability to "get it right." And so I say "nay."

Curiously, my interest in Politics was first stirred by a Democrat: JFK; and, more specifically, by his Inaugural Address, the hearing of which even now sends chills up my spine (I wore out a 33 RPM record I'd purchased that contained his entire speech). The sound of JFK's strong, energized voice—thick-laden with a Boston accent—ringing through the frosty January air in Washington in 1961 as he urged young persons in particular to join him in exploring a "New Frontier," reached my ears as if it were a trumpet call. Then a sophomore in high school, I suddenly felt an irresistible desire to become more politically aware. That urge has not waned since.

Surprisingly, it was Barry S. Goldwater and William F. Buckley Jr.—pillars of conservatism and the new darlings of the Republican Party—

who filled the void left in my heart by the assassination of John F. Kennedy. Goldwater, crusty, flamboyant and a son of the Arizona desert, and Buckley, debonair, articulate and a product of the Ivy League, had by then emerged as the leading proponents of a conservative movement that was spreading across the land. I read Goldwater's *The Conscience of a Conservative*, in which he laid out the tenets of the Conservative philosophy. I devoured Buckley's breakthrough book, *God and Man at Yale*, in which he cast aspersions on key ingredients of the liberal education he'd obtained in New Haven. I took out a subscription to Buckley's magazine, *National Review*. I joined Young Americans for Freedom (YAF). I rooted hard for Goldwater to win the presidential election of 1964; the manner in which he rattled the cage of the American public with his hard-line stand on Vietnam was precisely what the country needed as it vacillated over the appropriate course of action in Southeast Asia, I believed.

For a brief period a few years later Robert F. Kennedy—a Democrat—lit the same sort of emotions in me; I detected in RFK a passion similar to that demonstrated by Goldwater and Buckley, even though in Bobby Kennedy's case the eloquent arguments were always for government to lift the downtrodden out of their circumstances with the help of costly monetary handouts. Goldwater and Buckley countered just as vociferously that the only way for the less fortunate to get ahead was by breaking their dependence on assistance from the public sector. I can still picture Bobby Kennedy, his shirtsleeves rolled up, his words effecting the look of tears streaming down his face, championing the cause of the "have-nots" from the back of a train as it rumbled through the heartland, just as I can picture Barry Goldwater in his Air Force flight jacket proclaiming that it would be alright to employ nuclear weapons on the Communists in the pursuit of total victory and just as I can picture Bill Buckley raising his eyebrows in mock disbelief at an especially preposterous proposal issued by John Lindsey on curbing unemployment or improving municipal services during the zany race between them for mayor of New York City.

In the years since Bobby Kennedy was shot dead by Sirhan Sirhan, I have leaned farther and farther to the right, politically; nevertheless, it has often been the messenger more than the substance of what that person is saying that determines my "tilt." I may be an odd duck in this respect, in gauging my support for candidates—as they appear, grab the limelight for a little while, and then recede into the cornfield again (a la "Shoeless" Joe Jackson in the movie *Field of Dreams*). I may be one of the few persons professing to be a rock-solid conservative Republican who is sometimes tempted to partake of the apple from the tree as it is extended in friendship by a decidedly liberal and yet personally appealing Democrat. This has happened to me more than once.

The best example of my tendency to periodically stray from Conservatism's straight and narrow arose in the form of onetime New Jersey Sen. Bill Bradley's ill-fated run for the presidency. As "Blue State" as they come, Bradley had no business wooing me to his side of the fence. The trouble was, I'd been a diehard fan of his since his days as an All-America basketball player at Princeton. Early on, I'd read John McPhee's nifty little book *A Sense of Where You Are*, which described in vivid detail Bradley's uncanny intuitiveness when it came to knowing how and when to strike against an opposing defender (Bradley's amazing peripheral vision definitely played a role). *In A Sense of Where You Are*, McPhee related asking his father as they sat in the bleachers of the field house at Princeton to identify without any clues whatsoever the one player on the court who was destined for greatness. This wasn't a difficult deduction; Bradley's extraordinary abilities left little doubt. In terms of his foul-shooting prowess alone, in which he'd flawlessly sink shot after shot from a low contemplative crouch, Bradley was a rare specimen.

Bill Bradley went on to star for a world-championship New York Knicks team, which only intensified my admiration for him. He brought a rare cerebral element to the game. In his own book about his time in the NBA, *Life on the Run*, Bradley, who'd initially foregone a career in the professional ranks to continue his studies as a Rhodes scholar in England, talks about wandering into a gym one day—during his hiatus from the game. In the gym, he said, he picked up a basketball and started dribbling, feinting and shooting. The building was empty. The only sound, at first, was the echo of the ball bouncing off the floor. But then he heard the unmistakable roar of a crowd as he resumed a warm-up routine that had once been second nature to him. At that instant a voice told him it was time to return home: the NBA beckoned. His decision to follow that overture proved to be a momentous one for himself and the Knicks; united with the likes of Willis Reed, Earl Monroe, Walt Frazier, Dave DeBusschere and Jerry Lucas, Bradley became a vital cog in a machine that played to claps and cheers from the faithful several nights a week in Madison Square Garden.

In order to fit in as a member of a talent-rich Knicks squad, Bradley was required to perform a different role than he had in college. At Princeton, he was the Tigers' principal offensive weapon: a nearly unstoppable force who on any given evening was good for thirty or even forty points. His repertoire of shots and moves left foes—and the media—dizzy with awe. In New York, his skills were subordinated to those of the players who had been designated by Coach Red Holtzman to carry the attack for the Knicks. And so it was that the flashy scourge of the college ranks became the tempered and at times almost inconspicuous "fifth wheel" of the New York Knicks. Bill Bradley did not dominate the pro game as he had the college game; yet by accepting his place as a swingman who kept the Knicks' offense clicking with his constant rotation, sharp passing and sparse but still-effective shot making, he loomed as vital to the team's success as any other starter.

Bradley's downfall during his subsequent foray into national politics can be attributed to a blandness that exceeded even the tame aura he'd projected as a professional basketball player. His ultra-liberal views on everything from war to the workplace earned him plaudits in Trenton, New Jersey but these same positions left him no chance of picking up significant numbers of converts in Spartanburg, South Carolina, Austin, Texas, or Salt Lake City, Utah. Nor did his nerdy image, his diplomatic approach or his uninspiring touch as a speaker. With all of the color of a mathematician, he would never have been mistaken as a man who possessed the overwhelming charm, lashing tongue, spontaneous wit or obvious charisma of "Mayor Frank Skeffington" ("the last of the great big-city Irish political bosses") of Edwin O'Connor's *The Last Hurrah*, for instance.

Despite his disqualifying deficiencies, and my reservations about the particular "talk" he walked, I probably would have voted for Bill Bradley for president, if he'd gotten close enough to have earned a spot on the ballot. Such is the quandary I find myself in from time to time when it comes to politics, because of an eagerness to place stock in a candidate's character even if his line of thinking is flawed.

With the ascent of Ronald Reagan as titular head of the Republican Party, my allegiance to Conservatism was born anew. Seldom had I observed a man who rode so tall in the saddle; whose belief in America's greatness as "a shining city on a hill" matched my own; whose natural optimism about life I shared; whose faith in God's watchful presence set an example I found uplifting; whose devotion to good grooming I envied; whose love of humor and a mischievous but innocent prank I embraced; whose eyes, twinkling with anticipation of the bright morning to come, indicated to me that tomorrow would be a day I would not want to miss.

Today's politicians, Democrat and Republican alike (George W. Bush included) are a weak lot in terms of their ability to inspire confidence in the manner that Ronald Reagan did. The Pied Piper they are not; they are no more impressive than the awkward and dullard men who presently dominate boxing's heavyweight division: Sam Peter; John Ruiz; Shannon Briggs; Vladimir Klitchko. Political giants on the order of a Ronald Reagan and supercharged heavyweights in the class of a Joe Louis, a Rocky Marciano or a Muhammad Ali are in equally short supply.

On politics' current barren playing field, the nastiness between persons who harbor opposing points of view seems to have never been more conspicuous—or unnerving. It has led those who are not especially interested in the spectacle of political sparring to begin with the assertion, "I hate politics," and to wish the pursuit, in all of its seedy manifestations, would go away.

That is not going to happen anytime soon. Society is no more able to shed its political skin than a leopard is able to change its spots or a zebra to remove its stripes. In my opinion there is absolutely no likelihood that the "political animal" will go the way of the wild horse, the panther, the manatee or the Asian elephant and become an endangered species. Politics is firmly and irrevocably embedded in human nature. It has been with us from the start and is endemic to everything we do. It is a certainly a constant at the highest levels of government: in the give and take that occurs over bills up for consideration in Congress, in the jockeying for position that takes place in the back rooms and hallways of state houses across the nation, in the meetings of planning boards and conservation commissions from one end of the continent to the other as projects large and small are weighed and rejected or approved, in the selection of boys and girls who will suit up for Little League and youth soccer teams. Politics came into play when locals objected to the scheme for a McDonald's in Woods Hole, right here in Massachusetts; it is part and parcel of the ongoing clamor for the development of wind farms in the waters off Cape Cod. It was paramount in President Bush's decision to back off the "Dubai ports deal" when that idea produced a clamor of protest from all quarters; as a presidential spokesman put it, of the president's abrupt retreat in the face of certain defeat, "It was a tactical discussion at that point. Look, the president didn't fall off a turnip truck. He understood the political reality."

Politics breeds strange bedfellows, inside and outside the political arena; in commenting on the somewhat surprising cooling of off-hours relations between Supreme Court Justices Ruth Bader Ginsberg and Antonian Scalia—political opposites—talk-show guru Rush Limbaugh said, "They used to be best buds. He'd play the piano and she would sing!"

For all the ugliness it can provoke in behind-the-scenes backbiting and plotting and maneuvering and trading off of interests—at the water cooler, in the shower or sauna of the neighborhood "Y" or the fitness club, in the boardroom, on street corners, in coffee shops—politics is an unavoidable element of everyday existence. As is true of baseball's brush-back pitch and hockey's body check, it's not the prettiest gambit going. As the saying goes, "Politics ain't beanbag."

It's ours to embrace, however, for better or worse. The alternative is anarchy.

It is a rare thing, and a treat for fans of their shows on Worcester's WCUW, for deejays (left to right) Milton Cordiero ("Uncle Milty"), Jason James and Paul Lauzon to appear together under one roof as they did at a fundraiser at the South Quinsigamond Neighborhood Center in the winter of 2005-2006. Their collection of vintage Rock & Roll is exceeded only by their attachment to the music that defined a nation as it turned its eyes, in the 1950s, toward a more robust form of expression.

XV. Deejays

"Well gonna write a little letter
Gonna mail it to my local d.j.
It's a rockin' little record
I want my jockey to play
Roll over Beethoven
I gotta hear it again today"

"Roll Over Beethoven"
The Beatles
Partophone Records, 1963

From the moment they began their "conquest of America" in early 1964 until they recorded their swan-song album "Abbey Road," The Beatles were an international phenomenon. I had been out of high school less than a year and was already completely head-over-heels immersed in the craze known as Rock & Roll when The Beatles' plane touched down at JFK Airport in New York City. Their arrival sent shock waves across the land. The release of the single "Please Please Me" had officially ignited "Beatlemania;" their first No. 1 in the U.S., "I Want to Hold Your Hand," and an appearance on "The Ed Sullivan Show," would propel them faster along the road to immortality. Soon they would become known as "The Fab Four," and forty-five Top 40 hits would follow over a half-dozen years' span. Their eventual charting of twenty No. 1's in the U.S. would top even Elvis' seventeen. It had all begun unpromisingly enough back in England when four teenagers were running, biking and busing all over Liverpool in search of "new chords and old guitars and a half-decent drum kit and any gig at all" as one commentator has put it, but always, once they were together as a unit, *with a determination and a cockiness that led George Harrison to say, "We just had this amazing feeling of, 'We're going to do it.' " There were the five-set-a-night marathon sessions they performed in the rough-and-tumble bar-scene world of Hamburg, Germany, their appearances at lunchtime at a club called "the Cavern" in their native Liverpool (where they were discovered by Brian Epstein), their rejection by Decca Records, their signing instead with EMI-Partophone after they'd impressed Producer George Martin and the launch of their first single, "Love Me Do/P.S. I Love You." Strengthened by the songwriting collaboration that took place between John Lennon and Paul McCartney, their "mop tops," George Harrison's masterful guitar playing and Ringo Starr's adept drum work—not to mention their playfulness and cleverness with the public and the media, The Beatles gradually established themselves as Rock's greatest act. Their run lasted less than twenty years; it ended with Paul McCartney's announcement on April 10, 1970 that he was leaving the group. By the time John Lennon was murdered in New York City on December 8, 1980, however, all four had gone on to demonstrate their brilliance individually or as front men for other groups. The legacy of The Beatles is wrapped up in their music, in their films (e.g., A Hard Day's Night), in their involvement with the Maharishi Mahesh Yogi, in the strong influence exerted by Yoko Ono. As this is written only Paul McCartney and Ringo Starr are left, and they have gone their own way; yet the magic of The Beatles is forever.*

Take away the deejays and Rock & Roll would be lacking its primary advocates: the Perry Masons of the airwaves, the town criers of yesteryear, whose impassioned pleas on Rock's behalf are largely responsible for the hold the music took on America's youth half a century ago. Deejays were the ones who carried the songs to the masses, just as Johnny Appleseed spread seedlings west from Leominster, Massachusetts into Pennsylvania and Ohio. Deejays' zest for the artists and the music that now comprise the category known as "Oldies" was contagious; the heat they generated ignited a blaze that still burns—albeit a little less conspicuously than was the case at the outset. God bless 'em, one and all!

In the 1950s and 1960s, long before the advent of MTV and other channels on television devoted to the music industry, American teenagers' principal link to the songs of their youth was Radio and—more specifically—disc jockeys.

Just as we are still connected in life to education by teachers and books, to medical treatment by doctors, nurses, emergency rooms and hospitals, to the silver screen by actors and actresses, to travel by jets and cruise liners, to cooking by chefs and recipes and to style by fashion designers, clothing manufacturers and retail stores, the one thing that tied people my age to Rock & Roll during its infancy half a century ago were the radio stations and the DJ's to be found on the little AM radio that sat on a nightstand in the bedroom or that graced the dashboard of the family automobile.

So much has changed that most of today's kids would not be able to tell you, if queried on the subject as they are leaving the mall or the movie theater or the dance club, that AM—not FM—was the place to turn to, back then, for the latest hits. Mention the names of such legendary deejays as "Wolfman Jack," Alan Freed or even Casey Kasem (who came along later) to them and the reaction would undoubtedly consist of a blank stare or the response, "Huh?" They would know Dick Clark only because as the host of the nation's jazziest New Year's Eve party he is a seeming permanent fixture in our culture—on the order of the light bulb—but they would not be able to divulge the information that Dick Clark first attracted notice as the emcee of a record-hop program on WFIL in Philadelphia (the "gig" that led to an invitation to take over a local TV show called "Bandstand"). Or even that "Bandstand" (i.e., "American Bandstand") eventually became TV's longest-running music/variety program.

Unless they've seen George Lucas' *American Graffiti*, they also in all likelihood have never heard of Robert Smith: a.k.a. "Wolfman Jack." What a shame that they are unfamiliar with "The Wolfman," as many of us called him; until he fell dead in his wife's arms of a heart attack on July 1, 1995 upon returning home to North Carolina from a promotional tour for his autobiography *Have Mercy*, Wolfman Jack was one of Radio's most magnetic personalities. He had few equals in terms of impact in the history of the medium, and reveled in the fanfare his celebrity status had generated among an adoring public. He was inducted into the Radio Hall of Fame in 1996, and was referred to in records performed by The Guess Who ("Clap For The Wolfman") and Todd Rundgren ("Wolfman Jack").

As a youngster I delighted in being able to pick up the sounds of Wolfman Jack. Once known as "Daddy Jules" on WYOU-AM in Newport News, Virginia and as "Big Smith" on KCIJ/Shreveport, he fully emerged as a mega force in Mexico—initially with 250,000-watt XERF (1570 AM), which carried his raspy voice (and his trademark occasional impromptu howls) across much of the Southwestern U.S., and then with XERB-AM. By the time he returned to America with KDAY/LA, and then WNBC, and thanks in part to the exposure the Armed Forces Radio network gave him, he was an institution with the country's youth.

Locally in Endicott, New York, where I grew up, and on a wider scale in the 1950s and 1960s, deejays commanded attention that nearly matched in degree the acclaim accorded such prominent early stars of Rock & Roll as Little Richard, The Monotones, Little Anthony & The Imperials, Ritchie Valens, The Everly Brothers, Buddy Holly, The Big Bopper (J.P. Richardson), Fats Domino, Bill Haley & The Comets, Buddy Knox, Johnny Rivers and The Crests. From coast to coast, in backwater hamlets and main-drag big cities alike, deejays dominated AM radio's airwaves the way AM radio political talk-show hosts like Rush Limbaugh and Glen Beck do now.

Just as Limbaugh is the self-proclaimed president of "The Limbaugh

Institute for Advanced Conservative Studies" on the "EIB" (Excellence in Broadcasting) network today, with millions of listeners tuning in every afternoon, Casey Kasem was "King of the Countdown" from sea to shining sea from the moment his show debuted in July of 1970. Working as a deejay in his native Detroit and in Cleveland, Buffalo, San Francisco and Los Angeles, Casey Kasem was personally responsible for establishing the "American Top 40" as a rage of the teen set; his penchant for blending human-interest stories about individual artists with their songs (the "teaser lead-in bio") increased his stature all the more. Kasem's technique became a standard in the field and is still employed today by deejays like Scott Shannon of "the True Oldies" channel—although not nearly as extensively or effectively.

"Cruisin' " would never have evolved into a rite of passage for teens in virtually every corner of the country had it not been for AM Radio; searching the dial for the songs that had become ingrained in our consciousness—"The Great Pretender," by The Platters, "Little Darling," by The Diamonds, "Crying In The Chapel," by Sonny Till & The Orioles, "Rockin' Robin," by Bobby Day, "Duke Of Earl," by Gene Chandler—amounted to a treasure hunt. The practice of scouring the streets in an endless, tantalizing search for chicks was undertaken in a souped-up Corvette, Mustang or GTO (equipped with whitewall tires and sporting lots of chrome, polished to a sheen) whenever possible, and the banter between the occupants of the vehicle was always accompanied by the rhythmic thump of the sounds coming from the car's speakers, as The Penguins told the story of "Earth Angel," The Shirelles talked about "Soldier Boy," or The Kingsmen sang of "Louie, Louie." "Cruisin' " and playing the radio became intertwined, like bread and butter or hamburgers and French fries. Deejays became our next-best friends, ever eager to help us through the bittersweet years of dating, ever willing to serve as companions as we groped for a way out of the social maze in which we'd become lost.

AM Radio provided early Rock & Roll deejays like Alan Freed with an outlet to promote the music, and they tackled the task with the same sort of relish that P.T. Barnum employed to promote the circus. Within a year of going on radio with WJW/Cleveland, Alan "Moondog" Freed had become a sensation; he is credited with having introduced Rhythm & Blues featuring mostly black artists to white audiences, and with having coined the phrase "Rock & Roll."

By 1954 Freed was working at WINS/New York and giving artists like Bo Diddley, Chuck Berry and Frankie Lymon and the Teenagers wide girth. His fame continued when he moved to WABC/New York in 1958.

Although his career was ruined by his involvement in the payola scandal, Freed's foresight helped make Rock & Roll and the Top 40 permanent elements on the radio.

For an all too brief time too there was Murray "The K" Kaufman. Dubbed "the Fifth Beatle" by George Harrison, Kaufman rose to prominence in the mid-1960s on WINS-AM in New York City; he took many of his followers with him when he became one of the first FM "Rock jocks" with WOR-FM. His Rock & Roll shows, staged several times a year and featuring the likes of Bobby Vinton, Cream and The Who, further solidified his reputation as one of the music industry's premier personas.

Here in Central Massachusetts in those days, Worcester's WORC (1310 AM) was king, according to my friend Harry Berkowitz, whose love of music matches my own, and who has DJ'd weddings and other functions himself over the years. WORC's "House Party," hosted by Dick Smith, enjoyed a rabid patronage. Requests were a staple. "Where a record stood was based on the number of times it was requested," Berkowitz says, in recalling the period.

Another Worcester station, WAAB (1440 AM) used to set up a trailer from which "remotes" were done; once, Berkowitz says, "They set up next to my house."

Boston's WBZ (1030 AM) "had the best deejays and 50,000 watts of power. At night with a clear-channel signal, WBZ reached thirty states. They owned the airwaves!"

Berkowitz tells me WBZ boasted a lineup of deejays that any station would have been proud to claim: Carl DeSuze (a "laid-back Boston Brahmin type, with an English accent), Dave Maynard (whose blend of music and commentary "turned on housewives"), Jay Dunn (who'd end his stint with the words, "Put the coffee on, honey, I'm coming home"), Jefferson Kay (a rowdy character who used sound effects to maximum advantage), Bob Kennedy (a Folk fanatic), "Juicy Brucey" Bradley ("He was a nut...he would play excerpts from 'Screaming' Jay Hawkins and he did the 'Bruce Bradley Countdown'...he nicknamed The Beach Boys 'The Bleach Boys' because of their blond hair), Dick Summers in the wee hours ("He would get into stuff you didn't normally hear on the radio including Folk and Underground Rock like 'The Beat Goes On' by Vanilla Fudge").

Berkowitz remembers the days when WBZ broadcast live from Paragon Park at Nantasket Beach in Hull from June to September. "They'd bring in Freddie 'Boom Boom' Cannon (a locally popular and nationally prominent Rocker) from time to time."

"These guys were my idols," Berkowitz says. "As a kid I broadcast from my house. We wired speakers up under the porch. We had to improvise."

As was true around the country back then, "Record hops were big," Berkowitz says. "All the Catholic schools had them, and in Northbridge every Friday night after school was out there'd be a tennis-court record hop at the Community Center."

It is hard in 2006 to latch onto radio stations whose format allows for even a smidgeon of dedication to the Oldies; it is even more difficult today to come across deejays who are eager to promulgate interest in the artists and the songs of Rock & Roll's greatest decade (1956-1966). Upon first moving to Massachusetts I was tickled to find WROR in Boston (103.3 FM), which played the songs I wanted to hear. After a while, however, 103.3 FM tossed the vintage stuff out the window as if it was used bathwater; much to my chagrin, the station had apparently redefined "Oldies" as being mostly songs recorded after the mid-

1960s. Perturbed, and hungry for a channel to fill the void, I briefly switched my allegiance to the Classic Rock station; then I discovered WCRN in Worcester (830 AM): the nationwide "True Oldies" channel, as its official deejay voice, Scott Shannon, likes to call it (WCRN, regretfully, has since switched to talk).

Better yet, through a man who is both a business acquaintance and a friend—Joe Cutroni Jr., who is station manager at WCUW Community Radio (91.3 FM) in Worcester—I was introduced to "Rock & Roll Thursdays" and three deejays—Jason James, Paul Lauzon and Milton Cordiero—who appeared to me to be on a personal mission to sustain interest in the music I cherish. Between them every Thursday, James, Lauzon and Cordiero supply WCUW's audience with the kind of songs that put Rock & Roll on the map (NOTE: in the summer of '06, Jason James took a leave from his regular Thursday-morning slot to devote more time to establishing himself as a musician with groups like Jason James and the Bay State House Rockers).

That James, Lauzon and Cordiero are completely different personalities with varying approaches to their programs only adds to their charm. Jason James is much younger than his two counterparts and could be mistaken for Fabian or Elvis or Dion with his long wavy black hair, sheepish look and the quizzical expression that crosses his face as he ponders questions or comments. He also performs around New England with his own band, as lead vocalist and guitarist. He is determined to make it as a Rock & Roll star. When my wife and I saw him in action at the Blue Plate, a popular lounge in Holden, Massachusetts, in the winter of 2005-06, I asked him, before he took the stage, if he'd seen the movie *Walk The Line*, starring Joaquin Phoenix as Johnny Cash. "Four times!" he said. He then proceeded to open the show with a revved-up version of "Folsom Prison."

Blame in on the weird hours he keeps or the fact that as the early man he's spinning records before most working folks have drained their first cup of coffee, but James is much more muted in his approach than Lauzon and Cordiero. It is not unusual for him to reel off six, seven or more songs without any interruption. I'll often be wondering, as I drive to work, if perhaps he overslept or if the show is on autopilot this time around—so extended are the stretches in which the music keeps appearing sans commentary. Then he'll finally break in to say, in his casual, silky-smooth voice, "That was 'Muleskinner Blues.' "

James tends toward Country and Rockabilly. After seeing *Walk The Line*, he started feeding his listeners an almost steady diet of Johnny Cash material; much appreciated on my part, as it turns out, in that much of it I'd never heard (for great Johnny Cash tunes that are not in the mainstream, check out "The Night Hank Williams Came to Town" or "Tennessee Flat Top Box").

Milton Cordiero—the five o'clock guy, making him the evening drive-time deejay—is also the Doo Wop specialist.

"Uncle Milty" is a resident authority on Doo Wop; his ardor for Doo Wop shines through both in the wide range of material he plays for listeners—and his rapport with his audience. Never is this more apparent than when he comes back on the air after an interruption caused by technical difficulties of the kind that are a constant threat at WCUW. Given a second chance, Uncle Milty shifts from a mood of "I'm irritated" to one of "I'm exhilarated!"

A bastion of information on Doo Wop, Cordiero can be counted on to dig into his record library for all-time gems: "Yakety Yak," "Charlie Brown" or "Poison Ivy," by The Coasters, "The Stroll," by The Diamonds, "Bristol Stomp," by The Dovells, "Sh-Boom," by The Crew-Cuts, "Let's Go, Let's Go, Let's Go" or "Finger Poppin' Time" by Hank Ballard or "Blue Moon" by The Marcels. Cordiero's reverence for the tracks and artists he selects for air time is as much a constant as the baseball cap that he wears, behind the mike.

Of the three, Paul Lauzon is the zaniest, the most unpredictable and probably the most knowledgeable. His Thursday-morning show on WCUW, "Echoes of the Past," which directly follows Jason James' stint, is a love-in between himself and those who tune in every minute of the way (he can also be heard from 10:00 a.m. to noon on Fridays).

Lauzon's antics are largely responsible for the adoration people feel for him, and the feeling is mutual. "I love people!" he says. Born on the same day as his favorite artist, Elvis Presley (they were also discharged from military service on the same day, March 3, 1963, according to Lauzon) and strongly influenced in his inclinations towards becoming a deejay by both Alan Freed and Wolfman Jack, Lauzon takes to the air with all of the crackling energy of an electric current.

"I'm sixty-five years old and I still go like a bat out of hell," he said on April 14, 2006, after finishing his show, which he sometimes refers to as "Blasts from the Past." "My wife (Judith) keeps telling me I'm nuts, but it's what keeps me going."

Lauzon has been in radio since the age of thirteen and has been heard on such stations as WBBZ in Ponca City, Oklahoma and KLCL FM and MHLA in Lake Charles, Louisiana. Now, he is "always on the road," DJ'ing parties, weddings, graduation gatherings and other functions. He DJ'd all of the dances at Friendly House, a community place for kids in Worcester, for seventeen years.

Lauzon's "pretty good following" grew even larger after he got connected with rockitradio.net through the help of a buddy, Tom Ryan, who was well known for a Doo Wop diner he operated in Niagara Falls, New York. Thanks to rockitradio.net, anyone can now tune into Lauzon's "Echoes of the Past," regardless of where they live ("If you were in Ventura, California, you'd be picking it up on 99.1 FM," he says). At Rock-It Radio, Lauzon is a headliner along with such other personalities as Al "Cool Daddy" Smith and "Cool Bobby B." Smith is a retired school principal whose music collection numbers in the neighborhood of 5,000 LP's and 1,000 CDs. "Cool Bobby B." is rumored to have broken into a "day-timer" radio station's transmitter room way back in 1957, cranked the power up to 100,000 watts and broadcast Doo Wop throughout the Eastern seaboard. Cops responded to the incident but "the culprit" was never caught!

What people who listen to Paul Lauzon's "Echoes of the Past" get is a steady stream of Golden Oldies combined with Lauzon's often-whacky but always entertaining asides, which spew from his lips like a ball bouncing crazily down the driveway. The songs are straight out of yesteryear, like "Rockin' In The Jungle" by The Eternals, "Just A Little Bit Of Your Love" by Roscoe Gordon or "Twisting & Twanging" by instrumentalist Duane Eddy (to the accompaniment of Lauzon's shouts of "ah yeah, let's go, whew!") or a song by "the fabulous Bobby Freeman" ("fabulous" is one of his favorite words in

A showman through and through, Paul Lauzon DJ's a fundraiser for Worcester's WCUW (91.3 FM). He is a mainstay as well on the web (rockitradio.net).

describing the artists he elects to showcase on any given day). The next minute it could be Lauzon breaking in with remarks that tumble out of the sky like a meteor shower:

"I'm losing my voice, whadya know…yeow!"

Or, "We're two days now (Thursdays and Fridays)…I love it!"

Or, "Wo, hit it now…howdy doody!"

Or, "Good morning to the people of the Providence & Worcester Railroad, the folks at Wright Line on Grove Street and Aunt Rosie. Good morning to one and all!"

"Here's Jan & Dean…hiya, hello!"

Or, in putting in a plug for Milton Cordiero's evening drive-time Doo Wop show, "Don't forget 'Uncle Milty' tonight…we're rockin' and rollin' on 'CUW!' " or "We've got night-time boogie with Uncle Milty tonight, 5:00 to 8:00!"

His dedications, "For Nick over at Diamond Chevrolet, for Carol in Oxford," are laced with warmth that suggests a powerful fondness for his followers. One morning, for Carol, a frequent request-line caller, he played "Oh Carol," by Neil Sedaka.

Lauzon fans hold nothing back in blanketing him with praise, in the form of telephone calls, e-mails, letters, etc., for his enthusiastic approach, which hearkens back to the days of "old-time radio, which is what I loved," he says.

"I have been compared to Wolfman Jack," he says. "I've been told, 'if Wolfman Jack was alive, he'd be losing it because of you.' Once I got a call from Brooklyn, New York with a request! They said they had never heard anyone like me. I have no idea how they picked us up. It must have been a clear night!"

Having spent some time in retailing, Lauzon says "I treat my radio show like I would a customer in the store." He gives his audience everything he's got.

It all reverts back to the desire that arose in him when he was a teenager to be a deejay—an urge that was fed by the radio stations and the deejays he found on his AM radio as a boy: Worcester's WORC, WNEB (1230 AM, and featuring the voices of Jim Pansullo and Frank Avruch), WTAG, WAAB, Boston's WBZ, WINS/New York.

It intensified during his six years in the U.S. Army, which afforded him the opportunity to see Elvis live at Maguire Air Force Base and to meet such legends as Ricky Nelson and Jerry Lee Lewis. He remembers seeing "The Four Coins, The Four Aces and The Four Lads" at the old White City amusement park in Shrewsbury when WORC did shows from there; and, he says, "Some of us took Guy Mitchell around town in a limousine."

Lauzon has parlayed his love of Rock & Roll and his penchant for quirkiness into a show that his fans can't get enough of. With his unpredictability, one never knows what to expect. "People love that about me," he says. "They say, 'One thing about you, you can screw up royally but you have fun with it.' "

Lauzon will never be as large a commodity as his idols, Alan Freed and Wolfman Jack. But he knows he's had a significant impact, like many of the famous deejays, and is content with that.

"It's great and that's no lie," he told me. "All my life I wanted to be a deejay and no one gave me a break and WCUW comes along and look at me now!"

Police motorcycles are situated in a solemn line near a local church, during a funeral service; this image proves that, individually, or collectively, these special machines are always able to "make a statement."

XVI. Motorcycles

"Get your motor runnin'
Head out on the highway
Lookin' for adventure
And whatever comes our way"

"Born to Be Wild"
Steppenwolf
MCA Records, 1968

J ust as John Fogerty's and Mick Jagger's energy came to typify the success
that was achieved by the bands Credence Clearwater Revival and The
Rolling Stones, respectively, John Kay's verve is what propelled Steppenwolf
to almost instant acclaim among followers of Rock & Roll. With the release
of its debut album in 1968, a hard-edged bluesy piece of work, Steppenwolf
began to garner a fan base that would eventually number in the thousands
(and that would ultimately be dubbed "The Wolfpack," by way of tribute).
With the unleashing of its first big hit, "Born to Be Wild," in Dennis Hopper's
biker smash film Easy Rider, Steppenwolf became known for its no-holds-
barred style. John Kay was largely responsible for this approach.
Steppenwolf, he said, wanted to produce music that "worked on a gut level
but that also provided food for thought." The origins of Steppenwolf's raucous
sound can be traced all the way back to John Kay's own tempestuous childhood. Born Joachim Fritz Krauledat in the East Prussia area of Germany in
1944, he never knew his father, who was killed fighting in Russia before "John
Kay" was even a year old. He and his mother subsequently undertook two

harrowing flights, first to what would become Communist-controlled East Germany and then to West Germany. From an early age, John Kay was strongly influenced by the American Rock & Roll he heard on U.S. Armed Forces Radio—especially the shouts and screams of Chuck Berry and Little Richard. With the formation of the blues band Sparrow in Toronto after his emigration to Canada, John Kay found an outlet for the primal urges that would come to define such later Steppenwolf songs as "Born to Be Wild," "Magic Carpet Ride" and "Rock Me." Today, John Kay's name is inextricably linked with that of Steppenwolf even though the band broke up a long time ago and he went on to dabble with a solo career. When a "fake band" featuring some members of the original lineup materialized and started performing in clubs as Steppenwolf, John Kay's temper was aroused; in an effort to re-establish the band's good name, he formed "John Kay and Steppenwolf." Tours and albums followed, as did an annual weekend gathering of the faithful called "WolfFest" in the new band's adopted home base of Tennessee. For John Kay, the "Magic Carpet Ride" continues.

A motorcyclist's love affair with the open road cannot be dulled by the warnings of those who see danger lurking just around the next corner. Respect for the machine is of paramount importance, of course; so too the biker must be cognizant of the unique vulnerability to which he is exposed when he "saddles up." A need for caution in the face of the untenable situations in which he can find himself must therefore take precedence. With that, let "The Ride" begin.

The question asked over and over by those who do not ride is: "Why?" It is a query heard often too by others who confront danger head-on: bungee jumpers, parachutists, alligator hunters, mountain climbers, Indy-car drivers, matadors and long-distance swimmers.

Motorcyclists are just as accustomed as the aforementioned to being subjected to this proverbial inference that something has gone haywire in their brain: What other reason could there be than the onset of temporary insanity to explain the irrationality of an exercise that so often results in a maiming—or death?

There will never be a reconciliation of the two schools of thought. On the one hand there stands the belief by those who err on the side of caution that motorcycling is an inherently stupid undertaking; occupying the opposing ground is the conviction by those who have a bit of the adventurer in them that it makes all the sense in the world. The gap between these dramatically disparate viewpoints is as wide as the Grand Canyon; it is mirrored in the comment uttered by a friend of mine, Jim Marshall, who sells insurance products, when I mentioned to him that I had purchased a 1998 Yamaha V-Star. "Be careful!" he said.

Employing restraint has nothing to do with whether you live to see another day or are scrapped off the blacktop and sent to the county morgue, of course. With all of the variables that must be taken into account, there are no guarantees; every time a motorcyclist sets forth he is fully aware that something could go wrong. And yet, thumbing through the pages of the daily newspaper provides more than ample evidence that a rendezvous with an ill fate is a constant for one and all—"24/7," as they say. Even people who always wait for the walk signal when crossing the street, who drink Grape juice every morning, who lock the doors of their homes against burglars or rapists, who wear steel-toed boots and hardhats when working in a construction zone, who swallow two aspirin every night before they go to bed, who buckle themselves into the seat of a 737 for what they assume will be a routine flight to Orlando, who take the escalator rather than the stairs, who steadfastly refuse to be in a room in which they are subjected to second-hand smoke or who opt not to reside in areas that are prone to hurricanes, floods or earthquakes are continuously at the mercy of Circumstance. So it was, and always will be.

To cite a few examples from a typical day's datelines: in Missouri, a seventeen-year-old high school student lies in the woods for more than thirty hours, barely breathing, before being found; one of her teach-ers—a twenty-six year-old would-be professional wrestler (named "Samson," how bitterly ironic is that?) with whom she'd apparently had some sort of relationship—is charged with kidnapping and attempted murder…in Boston, the badly burned body of a nineteen-year-old woman is discovered in a forested section of Franklin Park, behind Lemuel Shattuck Hospital; apparently she had been killed first and then torched with an accelerant….in Singapore, at a conference, a leading American expert on the "H5N1" virus (bird flu) warns that the public can look for smuggled birds—not migratory birds—to carry a possibly mutated form of the deadly disease to the mainland, where it could then spread from human to human, potentially infecting and killing millions. On and on go the reminders that life is by its very nature an unexacting science, prone to pendulum-like swings and unexpected triumphs and tragedies.

Consider the sobering reality that one's next moment could be The End—and for reasons that are not even necessarily readily apparent, but rather totally unforeseen; the only conclusion that I can determine worth drawing from this picture is, "live!" Paint at the edge of Boston Harbor outside the Long Wharf Marriott if you are so moved as I have watched a man do, even though a cretin could come along and push you into the drink. Play the piano at a karaoke bar if that is your desire even though a drunken thug who doesn't like the music could wobble forward and whack you over the head with a beer bottle. Hike the Appalachian Trail if it has been a long-time ambition even though a mountain lion with an attitude might lurk in the shadows. Go on a cruise even if the boat might sink; rip apart an old shed even if there's the remote chance of running a rusty nail into your foot. Plant toma-toes in the back yard even though a rabid coyote might attack.

And ride motorcycles for an awakening of the senses that touches every fiber of one's being if the impulse arises, even if calamity might strike. Do it with the knowledge that the odds are no more unforgiving in that pursuit than they are in a host of other seemingly safer practices.

The tradeoff for persons willing to put themselves in harm's way on the seat of a flying machine is a freedom that is more nourishing to the soul—because of the absence of virtually all encumbrances—than even those civil liberties we Americans have long touted as our cherished God-given rights: freedom from want; freedom of speech; freedom of the will, etc. Indeed, one of the definitions of freedom put forth by Webster's is, "ease of movement or performance; facility." Webster's must have had a motorcyclist in mind in adding that particular description to the mix: the image, perhaps, of a solitary rider tooling along a placid country road with only the wind in his face looming as an impediment. In the Old West it might have been a cowboy, clad in britches and spurs; in the Techno Age it's a motorcyclist, wearing a black-leather jacket and boots. It is an elusive "high" that Billy Joel has referred to in song, with mention of "riding in the rain," and that Bob Seger has touted (he did so during a promotional interview for a January, 2007 show he would be doing at the DCU Center in Worcester), when he says, in response to a question, "Yeah, I still ride, with no windshield or anything like that. I enjoy being out in the elements."

It is a combination of savory thrills that compels some men (and women) to ride motorcycles; principal among these are the flow of power that is transmitted from the hands into the arms and shoulders and on through the body to the feet and toes whenever the throttle is given a twist, the distinctive roar of the "pipes" that can be heard by onlookers when the biker is making his pass through the neighborhood, the statement of protest that is implicit in the interaction between the "outlaw" rider and "compliant" society, the feeling of wanderlust that takes possession of the spirit at the outset of the journey. Destination unknown? Better yet! Riding in a pack? Absolutely!

The world is made up of leaders and followers, doers and slackers, realists and dreamers, heroes and villains; and—when it comes to indulgences like motorcycling—proponents and dissenters. The dissenters will never win over the proponents, their earnestness and noble intentions notwithstanding.

Acquaintances of mine who ride include Octavio, who owns a small printing business, Mark, who owns a gun shop and shooting range, Rocco, who owns a gentlemen's clothing store, and Mary, who works as a nurse in an area hospital.

All of them are regular folks with day jobs and largely ordinary lives except for when they slide onto the seat of their Harley, Kawasaki or Honda, strap on their helmet and charge off—rapidly climbing into third or fourth gear. At such times they are ready to take their walk on the wild side...full speed ahead and damn the torpedoes!

They would have it no other way. Neither would I.

XVII. Cigars

"I smoke old stogies I have found
Short, but not too big around
I'm a man of means by no means,
King of the road."

"King of the Road"
Roger Miller
Smash Records, 1965

Born January 2, 1936 in Fort Worth, Texas, Roger Dean Miller drifted from one town and one honky-tonk club to another in Texas and Oklahoma as a young man—determined to emulate the success of his boyhood idols Hank Williams and Bob Wills. It wasn't until he landed in Nashville in the 1950s that Roger Miller finally proved himself to be an incredible though initially under-appreciated talent both as a recording artist and songwriter (he also charmed people with his humor and wit). He co-wrote "Tall, Tall Trees" with George Jones; that tune was not an immediate winner, but was taken to No. 1 on the charts by Alan Jackson forty years later. Miller attracted huge notice in the 1960s with such crossover hits as "Dang Me" and "King of the Road." He considered his crowning achievement to be the writing of the score for the play "Big River," which opened on Broadway in 1985. Roger Miller died on October 25, 1993; he was posthumously inducted into the Country Music Hall of Fame in 1995.

The railroad-riding vagabond Roger Miller sings about in "King of the Road" is "a man of means by no

George Photakis is owner of The Owl Shop, a tobacco store on Main Street in Worcester that hearkens back to the days when the city's downtown teemed with storefronts and people. George no longer smokes cigars. "I lost my taste for them," he says. He hasn't lost his fondness for conversation, however, or his affinity for clothing (notice the handsome tweed jacket).

means." A cigar in the same man's hands, however, changes everything.

I have known a few cigar smokers, and indulge occasionally myself. One conclusion that can be drawn from this experience is that there are not, within the breed, too many who could be described as shrinking violets. Most, in fact, possess the same sort of chutzpah as those stalwart defenders of duty, honor and country who have emerged as fabled warriors down through the ages: David; William Wallace; Spartacus; Geronimo; Patton; Moshe Dayan.

Nor—though the pastime is a decidedly male pursuit—are their ranks confined to men who have achieved glory only in battle; on the contrary, whatever the circumstances, cigar smokers have invariably emerged as the best at what they do. It could involve commercial development, or the culinary arts, or painting. Some have even shifted gears to attain prominence in several areas of endeavor. Typical is Arnold Schwarzenegger, whose talents were first realized in body building, then film, and subsequently (as if he was reinventing himself yet again, in honor of the new millennium), politics. And for every Schwarzenegger there is a Groucho Marx, a Milton Berle (Comedy), a Winston Churchill (Statesmanship), an Arnold "Red" Auerbach (Professional Basketball), a William F. Buckley Jr. (Print/Broadcast Journalism) or a Rush Limbaugh (Talk Radio) as further proof that the man with the cigar clenched between his teeth is a force to be reckoned with. What stronger evidence could there be than my own unforgettable memories of the late Red Auerbach lighting up a "victory cigar" on the Celtics' bench in ceremonial celebration of still another win? Such impudence must have rankled opposing coaches to no end!

Having studied the species for some time, I am of the mind that it is not the cigar itself that gives cigar smokers an "edge." The cigar is merely a reflection of a confident, garrulous, positive nature with which they are imbued from infancy: cigar smokers are, almost without exception, natural-born achievers, extroverts and risk takers. The world is a far more interesting place for the gusto they bring to this difficult enterprise we call living (imagine how dull international relations would have been without Fidel Castro—for all his excesses and irrationalities—at the helm, in Cuba). In a pinch, with the contest, or the fight, on the line, I'd want a cigar smoker by my side.

I was introduced to cigars back in the 1960s. The individual who did the honors—Edward W. Plaisted—was then the sports editor of the now-defunct *Sun-Bulletin*, a feisty tabloid newspaper published in Binghamton, New York. Plaisted penned a column that was as notorious for its capacity to send readers into a rage as it was for producing typos (he was a horrendously bad speller).

At the time, a number of sportswriters scattered around the country had attained near-cult status for their slickness in rendering opinions that warmed people's blood to a fast boil. Employing humor, sarcasm, a biting wit and a seemingly infallible grasp of their subject matter, such luminaries as Arthur Daley (*The New York Times*), Dick Schaap (the *New York Herald American*), Jimmy Cannon (the *New York Journal American*), Shirley Povich (*The Washington Post*) and Jim Murray (the *Los Angeles Times*) hammered points home like laborers driving spikes into railroad ties (the irascible Jimmy Cannon even had the audacity to start each new column with the words, "Nobody asked me but…").

Ed Plaisted was every bit as outrageous with the commentary he offered for consumption as his bigger-name peers. Nothing pleased Plaisted more than getting folks riled up.

Plaisted was also oblivious to criticism. It rolled off him like water. Once, when he was booed by some fans upon walking into the gymnasium at Binghamton Central High School for suggesting, in print, that the BCHS basketball team change its nickname from Bulldogs to "Puppydogs"—because of consistently woeful play on its part, which had resulted in a string of defeats —he returned to the office convinced that the avalanche of derision that greeted his entrance was further evidence of the BCHS followers' frustration with their hapless charges, not an indication of their disgust with him! Hard as it is to believe, this event proved to be a precursor; Plaisted would later raise a ruckus in Beloit, Wisconsin by launching a campaign that called for tossing out the moniker by which University of Wisconsin's sports teams were identified ("Badgers") and substituting one that more appropriately mirrored what the state was famous for ("Holsteins").

Slightly rotund, jovial, red-cheeked and prankish, Plaisted would never have stooped to the level of plucking a half-consumed "stogie" off the sidewalk (they were so-identified, according to Webster's, because they were the preferred choice of drivers of Conestoga wagons). For Plaisted, only the better smokes would suffice. Preferably a Robert Burns.

Robert Burns cigars came wrapped in cellophane, and were further sealed for freshness in a metal canister. Plaisted would buy them in the lobby of the old Arlington Hotel (as grand a lodging facility as ever existed, in its heyday). He would break one out for his personal enjoyment after his usual mid-evening meal at the Little Venice, on Chenango Street, the Celeste, on Court Street (both of which were within walking distance) or—occasionally—at Jimmy Cortese's place on Robinson Street (uptown). He treated his cigars as if they were something to truly savor: the equivalent of a German torte, perhaps, or a French truffle. After touching a match to the tip of the cigar and taking several long pulls on it to ensure that it was properly "prepped," he would hold the cigar delicately between the forefinger and middle finger of his right hand and blow smoke slowly toward the ceiling— sometimes in ringlets. I detected in this affectation an assumed reverence for the object of his attention that would have made the good preacher Dr. Norman Vincent Peale proud, were it directed toward Redemption rather than Self Aggrandizement.

His patronage of those fine restaurants reflected Plaisted's perpetual pursuit of "The Good Life." He was as devoted in his quest for gratification as the explorers De Soto and Magellan were in their relentless search for undiscovered territories.

Plaisted would also fire up a cigar around midnight, after we'd put another edition of the paper "to bed." At those moments, he would lift his feet above him in a semi-reclined position and expound on a variety of topics; the authoritative air he projected during such conversation was not dissimilar from that I'd read as being evoked by Socrates and Samuel Johnson when they held court with their "students." This aura of infallibility was reinforced whenever Plaisted slapped his wooden yardstick on the desk with a loud smack to emphasize a particularly salient point he had just made. The glow in his face then, and the wink that came with it, were as if to say, "Have you ever encountered such absolutely erudite discourse in all your life?"

Married with no children, Plaisted loved to banter and tease (waitresses came in for their share of flirtatious ribbing). When talking to his wife on the telephone, from the office, he would playfully greet her with a deep-throated "Grrrrrr!" (I surmised, based on the dirty small talk that ensued, that she encouraged this behavior).

He was schedule-oriented. His days and nights were well-ordered ones, and designed with a degree of pampering built in. He typically slept late. He always showed up at the YMCA before work for a game of 3-on-3, 4-on-4 or 5-on-5, throwing his weight (and his elbows) around, maliciously, for effect. After showering, he always slipped into a nicely pressed cotton shirt and snappy tie, with a dab of musk applied for effect. At seven o'clock, he always took an hour (or more) for dinner. Nothing got in the way of these rituals, least of all a job.

He was a creature of habit, and one of his habits was to project an air of superiority over cronies and acquaintances. He relished his role as "King Tut" (my initial duties as a sportswriter in his employ were to fetch coffee for him from a café just around the corner, to run to the Western Union office minutes before deadline for the results of the "pony" races at Monticello, Vernon Downs and Pocono Downs and to pull box scores off the UPI wire so that they could be "set" on the linotype machine; there were no live game stories to be covered and written up until I'd proven I could complete these simple chores to his satisfaction). And yet he maintained a profound regard for his underlings' welfare; when, one afternoon at the height of the Vietnam War, in

deciding to check out my various "options" for military service, I drifted toward the U.S. Marines Corps recruiting office in a federal building in Binghamton, Plaisted, following along, shouted, with horror in
his voice, "Don't go in there!"

I have never met a cigar smoker who was anything less than a fire-
brand. Or who will be remembered as anything less than a star. To par-
aphrase Grantland Rice, the greatest sportswriter of them all: "For
when the One Great Scorer comes to write against your name, He
marks—not that you won or lost—But what you smoked when at the
game."

Through his column in the *Boston Herald* and his weeknight talk show on WRKO (680 AM), Howie Carr excoriates all sorts of people who could be considered public threats (or at least nuisances): crooked or nincompoop politicians (he calls them "hacks"), illegal immigrants, welfare cheats, child abusers, imposters, murderers, rapists, thugs, gypsies, tramps and thieves. One of Carr's frequent targets—former Massachusetts House Speaker Tom Finneran (a radio colleague of Carr's and a convicted felon) turned the tables, so to speak, by suggesting to Massachusetts Gov. Deval Patrick, on the air, that Patrick, Finneran and Carr take a ride in the governor's Cadillac "and only two will come back." Finneran's "hit-job" remark was intended as a joke but Carr took "Howie-ling" offense. The March 5th front page of the Herald, shown here, captured the entire brouhaha, as Carr immediately called for Finneran to be thrown in prison for violating the conditions of his "unsupervised probation." The episode is one of the few times Carr has been upstaged as a "bad boy." Well-versed on current events (including the exploits of the University of North Carolina basketball team, which represents his beloved alma mater), he walks fearlessly where others fear to tread. By employing an entertaining and mesmerizing mix of indignation, disgust, braggadocio, humor, charm and nerve, "Howard Lawrence Carr" has developed a huge audience of listeners. They hang on his every word; many of them, when they call in, affectionately address him as "Captain." With every utterance—written or spoken—he seems to be saying to his followers, "I will defend a way of life in America that is under siege until I can no longer draw breath to do so." Indeed, he has referred to himself as "the last American dishwasher." In his interactions with the public at signings for his book *The Brothers Bulger* and in other encounters, he is a perfect gentleman—full of sweetness and courtesies; when wrongdoing rears its ugly head, however, the gloves come off and there is serious hell to pay.

136

XVIII. Bad Boys

"I may drink too much and play too loud
Hang out with a rough and rowdy crowd
That don't mean I don't respect
My mama or my Uncle Sam
Yes sir, yes ma'am
I may be a real bad boy
But baby I'm a real good man"

> "Real Good Man"
> Tim McGraw and The Dancehall Doctors
> Curb Records, 2003

Being the son of a famous major league ballplayer is sort of like living in the shadow of the Sphinx, but Tim McGraw has managed to grab his own share of the spotlight and then some. In fact, within a mere ten years or so of crashing the Country scene in the early 1990s, he had succeeded in surpassing Garth Brooks as the most popular male singer in the medium. Credit goes to hits he churned out with assembly-line proficiency, including such chart smashes as "Indian Outlaw," "Don't Take the Girl," "Down on the Farm" and "Refried Dreams." Three of my personal favorites are "I Like It, I Love It," "Live Like You Were Dying" and of course "Real Good Man." "Real Good Man" could be viewed as Tim McGraw's testament to his occasional flirtation with wrongdoing (as reflected by a celebrated scuffle with police officers in which he and tour mate Kenny Chesney got involved in 2004) (in an example of better judgment, he married Faith Hill). In some respects Tim McGraw is "a chip off the old block" even though it was years after his birth (on May 1, 1967, in Delhi, Louisiana) before he found out that Tug

McGraw—a flamboyant and zany but gifted relief pitcher for the Philadelphia Phillies and New York Mets—was his father. Tim McGraw apparently inherited his dad's industrious nature; when Tug McGraw died of brain cancer in February of 2004 (at Tim McGraw's home), former Phillies Manager Larry Bowa said, in tribute, "he epitomized what Philadelphia is all about" with his hardworking and dedicated approach to his job. It was Tug McGraw who coined the phrase "You Gotta Believe" as "the Miracle Mets" of 1969 shocked sports fans by winning the National League pennant and then the World Series. Tim McGraw might have followed in his footsteps; he attended Northeast Louisiana State University on a baseball scholarship. Fortunately for music lovers, he picked up a guitar instead.

Throughout history—on the stage, in the literary world, in the sports arena, in politics, in medicine and science and in the everyday workplace—"bad boys" have been an object of fascination; typically, they have also left a larger mark than "nice guys." We have almost come to expect from our showmen that they exhibit a rogue-like character; in their accommodation of this small request on our part, they fulfill our fantasies—and realize their own destiny. "Boys" who know how to be "bad" without crossing the line into obnoxiousness or criminality earn praise and respect that is richly deserved, in my opinion.

A little bit of what I call "the nasty" goes a long way in determining a person's capacity to influence those around him. It can be an asset rather than a liability, and an instrument of persuasiveness that alters the scheme of things in a positive way. This has been the case since the beginning of time.

Cher would certainly not be as nearly as potent a force in the sphere of entertainment were it not for a touch of "the outlaw" in her, for example; I once sat in the high seats at the arena in Worcester with a set of binoculars focused on her lusciously exposed midriff and thighs in an attempt to pick up a glimpse of a celebrated tattoo (the mission was accomplished). Cher's inclination to flaunt her sensuality acts as an accelerant, not a retardant.

Matt Peloquin, of Bellingham, who met Cher at a party for the launch of the movie *Stuck On You*, says sweetness typifies her every move; while this may be true, it is her willingness to let the naughty girl emerge that heightens Cher's appeal to millions of fans.

A high school dropout, Cherilyn LaPierre rose to stardom on the strength of a sonic-boom-like voice that first caught attention when she sang backup on such Phil Spector-produced classics as The Crystals' "Da Doo Ron Ron," The Ronettes' "Be My Baby" and The Righteous Brothers' "You've Lost That Lovin' Feelin.' " What hoisted her career upward, however, especially among male admirers, was an inclination to "tease" in a largely wholesome and yet provocative and titillating manner. It's the same formula that has worked for countless performers who preceded her including Marilyn Monroe, Bridget Bardot, Elizabeth Taylor, Farah Fawcett and Sophia Loren. A picture of Cher that appears with the liner notes to her CD "The Very Best of Cher" is a perfect example of how she counterbalances "good" and "evil" for maximum commercial effect. She is made up to resemble an angel, complete with wings. She is sitting on a bed of clouds. And she is totally naked except for the long hair—bleached snow white—that cascades from her head down over her shoulders, covering her breasts.

Her fetish for outlandish costumes defines Cher; it is what's underneath, though, that interests guys most.

I can still see Cher on a ship with a horde of hungry and horny sailors thunderously clapping their approval as—half-dressed—she belts out the hit "If I Could Turn Back Time" (a track so rousing from start to finish that it has been described by Kurt Loder as "a shout-along anthem").

Had Cher chosen to remain a "plain Jane" upon embarking on a career as an entertainer, she would have made much less of a splash.

Like Cher, such comparable sex sirens as Madonna, Paris Hilton, Bridget Fonda, Halle Berry, Rachel Hunter, Tina Turner, Nicole Kidman, Sharon Stone and Paula Abdul regularly employ a dab of "wickedness" in either their dress or their public persona in an attempt to garner attention—and curry favor. The best of them exercise this gambit judiciously, and with great aplomb. They never surrender their essential innocence; they merely use a shadowing of disobedience to blur the edges of the image just enough to establish themselves as refreshingly individual and slightly naughty.

Accomplished men, regardless of vocation, have invariably demonstrated a similar proclivity for "breaking the rules" (or at least "stretching" them) in order to create an aura of unmistakable virility in the eyes of a watchful public. Generally speaking this approach has paid dividends for those who push the boundaries—male or female. "Nice guys" may not always finish last, but they seem to rank lower than "bad boys" in the pecking order for their failure to arouse emotions—and so are shoved to the side as if they were a bruised piece of fruit. Everyone has heard of Norman Mailer, who is perceived by thousands to be a charter member of the Bad Boys Club; how many people, however, can say they are aware of the late Eudora Welty? Just as gifted a writer, and a Pulitzer Prize winner, Eudora Welty's shortcoming was the demure profile she kept; a near-lifelong resident of her beloved Mississippi, she was the very model of Southern gentility. Mailer, in contrast, has been the poster child for big-city ribaldry. Hence his frequent mention in the gossip columns of the New York tabloids, for one supposed misstep after another. Had Eudora Welty possessed a seamier demeanor, like Mailer does, she would have seen her stock rise as a literary force.

The ones who adopt a tougher facade—those individuals who inspire as much for the moxie they bring to life as for their talents in their selected field—appear to fare better in the workplace and outside of it too, at least in terms of provoking reaction and in demonstrating staying power.

Ernest Hemingway most assuredly belongs in the ranks of people who have elected to pursue a course in which indecorum trumps politeness, with beneficial results. In implementing this strategy, Hemingway appeared to realize with the astuteness of a Madison Avenue marketing marvel that machismo sells. And so Hemingway honed a reputation as an untamable stallion through his adoration of lion hunts, bullfights, boxing, drinking, gunplay, war and irresistibly beautiful women (not necessarily in that order); he pursued these interests with an unfettered bloodlust. In doing so, he showed no concern for his own personal safety. This approach lifted the stories he penned to a loftier place; it also made him seem like a titan among midgets on the shelves of bookstores around the nation.

In a revealing segment of his marvelous biography *Hemingway*, Kenneth S. Lynn describes an episode of fisticuffs that occurred between Hemingway and the poet Wallace Stevens after the latter told Hemingway's sister Ursula that her brother was "a sap and not really very much of a man." Hemingway, who fancied himself an able boxer even though he was slow of foot and lacking good coordination and reflexes, and who'd studied fighters his entire life, immediately sought Stevens out. They squared off in the "rainy twilight" of a Key West night. Although Stevens stood six-foot-two and weighed two hundred twenty five pounds, Hemingway knocked him down three times. Stevens landed one punch flush on Hemingway's jaw but broke his hand in the process. As Lynn recounts the incident, Hemingway agreed to go along with Stevens's "official account" that he had hurt his face and hand falling down a flight of stairs. After Stevens left town, however, Hemingway, in a triumphant mood, divulged the details in a letter to a friend, Sara Murphy. In gloating over his pugilistic prowess, Hemingway belittled Stevens's own efforts, saying, "I hope he doesn't brood about this and take up archery or machine gunnery."

No one ever ran against the grain with greater élan—or effectiveness—than the actor Mickey Rourke, who starred in the 1986 scorcher of a film *9 1/2 Weeks*. Boxer, carouser, biker, playboy and general unrepentant hell raiser on screen and off, Rourke has filled the role of a bad-ass dude in a number of B-grade flicks. Reviewers have generally dismissed all of them—including *Wild Orchid* and *Barfly*—as worthless pieces of trash (I, however, love them precisely because they appeal to my sleazier impulses).

In *9 1/2 Weeks*, in his part as Wall Street investor John Grey, Rourke "educates" divorced art gallery owner Elizabeth McGraw (Kim Basinger) on the finer points of voyeuristic behavior. Together, they tread an increasingly dangerous path—as their sexual escapades become more and more over the top (in perhaps the most memorable scene—and one that was panned by critics as incongruous—they copulate under a downspout of freezing New York rainwater; in another, Basinger does a strip to the wail of Rocker Joe Cocker's "You Can Leave Your Hat On").

9 1/2 Weeks bombed at the box office but became a hot seller on the video market and something of a cult classic. As for Mickey Rourke, his rap as a troublemaker even got him blackballed in Hollywood for a while; he finally wormed his way back into the good graces of screenwriters, producers and directors by toning it down a bit.

H.L. Mencken—"the Sage of Baltimore," newspaperman, magazine editor, pontificator on the American language, author, stylist, iconoclast—would probably have liked Mickey Rourke for his uncouthness, if nothing else. Though far more erudite in my estimation than Rourke, Mencken (who also took a dim view of actors) possessed the same enthusiasm as Rourke about the prospects of stirring up a hornet's nest.

During what has been termed "a long, loud and loquacious life" in which he squeezed every bit of substance out of the day and then washed the heat and dust of his exertions down with bucketfuls of Pilsner at night, Mencken rendered observations on a startling variety of scenes and situations in and around the Port of Baltimore and even farther "across the fruited plain" (to cop the reference Rush Limbaugh employs in describing America). One minute Mencken would be lampooning Marriage, the next Government or Christianity or Institutions. Mencken became, as it has been said, "the terror, first of Baltimore, then of the Republic." His diatribes were indisputably the statements of a journalist who possessed the same degree of pedigree as the race-horses Citation, Secretariat and Whirlaway. Mencken plunged forward in a headlong rush; no winner of the Kentucky Derby (or Baltimore's own The Preakness, for that matter) ever charged down the back-stretch at Churchill Downs with nostrils flaring any more fiercely than Mencken did when he was on a roll at the typewriter.

The same man who dismissed New York City as "a third-rate Babylon" presented us with some of the most pungent quotes ever issued: statements that must leave those to whom they were directed still squirming in their graves. A sampling:

"A church is a place in which gentlemen who have never been to heaven brag about it to persons who will never get there."

"A good politician is quite as unthinkable as an honest burglar."

"A cynic is a man who, when he smells flowers, looks around for a coffin."

"A man may be a fool and not know it, but not if he is married."

Mencken had a low but not preposterously erroneous opinion of Mankind and Life. In four short words he summed up his "take" on the futility of human pretentiousness: "Time stays, we go."

If H.L. Mencken is my all-time No. 1 idol for barely constrained irreverence, *Boston Herald* Columnist and WRKO Radio Talk Show Host Howie Carr—who revels in the stature he has acquired as "Boston's bad boy" (as he is so identified on WRKO)—is a close second.

Over the years, in print and across the airwaves of 680 AM, Howie Carr, in the style of the late Jerry Williams (a WRKO legend and a man he looked up to), has considered it his personal mission to lambaste the sad sacks who portray themselves as holier than thou, wiser than Solomon, mightier than Caesar or simply smarter than the rest of us. High on his list are Democrats, and chief among these are anyone with the name Kennedy and right after them John Forbes Kerry. His unmerciful bashing of the Kennedys and "John 'F'ing' Kerry" allows them no time off for "good behavior" and no reprieve for legitimately commendable efforts they have expended on the legislative front. That is why, in early June of 2006, after Congressman Patrick Kennedy (Sen. Ted Kennedy's son, whom Howie Carr derisively refers to as "Patches") got in an automobile accident and was "let off the hook" by D.C. police even though he was apparently strung out on drugs, alcohol (or both), Carr speculated that "Daddy" was probably disappointed in that the incident didn't involve "water, a bridge—and definitely not a woman" (an obvious reference to Mary Jo Kopecne and Chappaquidick).

Days later Carr's rain of fire on the target had not abated; as "Patches" went public with an apology, an explanation and a vow never to touch booze again (after initially asserting that he hadn't been drinking), Carr ranted, "Say it isn't so, 'Patches.' We thought you were sober as a judge!" He deplored the fact that "Patches" had been allowed to squirm free of consequences. "The case was fixed," Carr said. "Now he's willing to cooperate with authorities. It's outrageous that he's getting this kind of pass!"

Carr's nickname for Patrick Kennedy's father (and the Commonwealth's senior senator) is "Fat Boy." This is only a slight variation on the tag he put on former Massachusetts State Sen. Matt Amorello (one of the few Republicans Carr has chosen to repeatedly vilify), who went on to head up the Massachusetts Turnpike Authority. For his part in the oversight of the Big Dig, the most expensive (and wasteful) public-works project in U.S. history, Carr dubbed Amorello "Fat Matt" (I always say "Ouch" when Howie Carr rips into Amorello, who used to live just up the road from me and who is a friend of mine).

Like H.L. Mencken, Howie Carr has demonstrated that a degree of "piss and vinegar" layered over an otherwise accommodating and even winsome personality can turn a lamb into a lion. Switching "the nasty" on and off as needed is the way "bad boys" relegate the "nice guy" in them to the sidelines in order to put their fiercest self on the playing field and win the game. Nine times out of ten, the strategy works.

The balance he achieves between politeness and beastliness is what makes Howie Carr such an irresistible spokesman for arguments espoused by "the right wing," and such a popular celebrity—in my judgment. Everyone who tunes in to "The Howie Carr Show" appears to relish the blend of braggadocio, humor, indignation and pungent observation he brings to the task. They seem to enjoy his modus operandi even when in disagreement with his thesis.

The image Howie Carr has crafted as a person who is no sufferer of fools, whose mouth waters at the mention or the sight of doughnuts, bacon cheeseburgers, rib-eye steaks or Kelly's roast-beef sandwiches (or any meal from Hearth 'N' Kettle, a restaurant chain he has done commercials for), who suggests that he rules his wife and daughters at their home in Wellesley with an iron fist, who has no sympathy for homosexuals, illegal aliens and freeloaders and who is as miserly as Shakespeare's Shylock (while at the same time supposedly pulling down a six-figure salary) sparks some of the show's most hilarious responses from listeners. These often surface during a five to ten-minute segment of the broadcast called "The Chump Line," and provide ample verification that "a bad boy" who is a "real good man"—as opposed to one who is just downright offensive (like the discredited Don Imus)—can command deserved attention, and respect.

"The Chump Line" airs during the evening commute, just after the five o'clock hour. It is not unusual for callers to use this forum to pick up on something Carr has said, or some situation in the news, with a sophomoric but catchy poem or a song. It is also not uncommon for them to sign off their message with a derogatory reference to the host, usually ending with the syllable "MO" (an apparent takeoff on "homo") as in "you $700,000-a-year fat-bastard sexist-MO, you"—just for the fun of it, mostly. The tone of these "rebuffs" usually makes it obvious that genuine affection—not deep-seated animosity—is the provocation for the call.

Once, for example, Carr complained that oatmeal-raisin cookies (which he doesn't care for) were put out in equal numbers to choco-late-chip cookies (which he loves) at a signing for his bestseller book *The Brothers Bulger*, saying, "Who eats oatmeal-raisin cookies? They're like coconut-flavored doughnuts at Dunkin' Donuts, that just sit and never get bought." The next day's "The Chump Line" featured an inspired defense of coconut-flavored doughnuts from a caller, who summed up his remarks by referring to Carr as a "coco-MO."

Having seen Howie Carr up close and personal at a bookstore in Winchester (just north of Boston) during an autograph session for *The Brothers Bulger* in March of 2006, I observed an individual who possesses all of the appropriate social graces: a man so inclined toward deferential greetings and common courtesies ("good afternoon, ma'am" or "nice to meet you" or "thanks to all of you who brought food today") that you would think he was a doorman at a high-class hotel like The Westin at Copley Place—not a modern-day dragon slayer.

Make no mistake, however: this educated and cultured gentleman is a bad boy with an attitude when the lights go on. His recognition of the need to sometimes "bust in and slit throats," as Mencken would have put it, is what sets Howie Carr apart from the "nice-guy" talk-show hosts whose anger or disgust seldom reaches measurable levels. In this regard he towers over even the late, esteemed David Brudnoy of WBZ (1030 AM) in Boston, whose voice rarely rose above the level you would encounter in polite conversation, and Peter Blute of WCRN (830 AM) in Worcester, who can't quite bring himself to go for the jugular.

In telling illegal immigrants to "go back to your third-world hell hole, we don't want you," Howie Carr will tout himself as "the last American dishwasher." In walking the line between savageness and lightheartedness, which he does with such dexterity, he will tell a defender of illegal immigrants in one breath that is laced with fury, "Screw!" and then shout in the next with an obvious reach for levity, "This is one 'gringo' that ain't going to be pushed around anymore!"

That Howie Carr long ago achieved enough credits to earn induction into "The Bad Boy Hall of Fame" is apparent in a statement George Keverian, the late Speaker of the House in Massachusetts, made, when he said, "If Howie Carr was ever murdered, there would be enough suspects to fill the Fleet Center!"

XIX. Boston

"I'm gonna tell you a story
I'm gonna tell you about my town
I'm gonna tell you a big,
bad story, baby,
Aww, it's all about my town"

"Dirty Water"
The Standells
Tower Records, 1965

The 1960s Los Angeles garage-style rock band The Standells made up for their all-too-brief moment in the limelight with a short string of clamorous songs that caught the attention of the public; most notably, of course, "Dirty Water," a captivating ditty that created the distinct but erroneous impression that the group was from Massachusetts. "Dirty Water," a remarkable expression of an individual's unabashed love for a place despite its obvious blemishes, was written by The Standells' producer Ed Cobb. Its words were made famous by lead singer/drummer Dick Dodd (a former Mouseketeer). It reached No. 11 on the Billboard charts in June of 1966. It became a standard after every Boston Red Sox and Boston Bruins home win. For a few years The Standells seemed to be headed for superstardom; Rolling Stone magazine even went so far as to describe the group as possessing "Stones-like greatness," punctuated by a "vintage AM-radio snarl." The release of "Dirty Water," their first hit single, was followed by a few other songs that grabbed something of a foothold: "Riot On Sunset Strip," "Sometimes Good Guys Don't Wear White" and "Why Pick On Me."

The Boston Celtics could not have a better ambassador than former Providence College star Ernie DiGregorio, who is pictured here advocating for both the game of basketball and the merits of education during an appearance at a school in Worcester in 2002. Schoolchildren gathered in a hallway for the event were captivated by Ernie's warmth and wit, and dazzled by his Harlem Globetrotter-like ball-handling prowess (at Providence, he won the Joseph Lapchick Memorial Trophy as the best collegiate player in the U.S.). "Ernie D" is a classic symbol of the drive for excellence that has historically typified the Celtics organization—and the city of Boston.

Suddenly Guitarist Tony Valentino and Organist Larry Tamblyn's The Standells were an item; they appeared in a couple of low-budget films and even made a heavily promoted showing on the sitcom "The Munsters" in the episode "Far Out Munster." At the height of their popularity they had "one foot in LA's Sunset Strip and the other in Boston's River Charles," as one observer has put it. By 1968, however, they had broken up (many years later they managed to reunite, and they performed at the second game of the 2004 World Series at Fenway Park). Thanks to "Dirty Water," they will always own a piece of American history.

"Frustrated women" who "have to be in by twelve o'clock." That's the Boston of Puritan times, a city that still adheres to a smattering of strict religious codes of conduct and certain prim social graces all these years later. "Boston, you're my home…" a lot of people share that sentiment. I'm one of them.

It is possible to feel an affinity for a place even before actually having set eyes upon its outline, or having put feet down within its bounds. Such is the magnetism of some locales that the pulse quickens at the very thought of one day going there in the flesh; until this occurs, dreams are all that can carry forward the hope of a for-real visitation.

Dorothy had her visions of Oz, Columbus had the picture of a New World in his mind, Dickens imagined with the incessant longing of young adulthood what it would be like to come across the Atlantic to America.

In my own case a fascination for the city of Boston started to develop a full thirty years prior to my trek east from Binghamton, New York to "the Hub" in the spring of 1985 to accept a position as editor of a group of weekly newspapers. By that time the hunger in my belly to follow my own yellow-brick road to the land of milk and honey (otherwise known as "the Athens of America") had reached a ravenous state, growing ever more intense as the miles clipped past and the flat farmland of Leatherstocking country gave way to the blue-green swatches of mountains known as the Berkshires—in western Massachusetts. With the sight of each overhead sign along the Massachusetts Turnpike (simply "the Pike" to native New Englanders), signaling an exit coming up for Stockbridge, Lee, North Adams, Westfield, Springfield, Amherst, Palmer, Sturbridge, Auburn, Worcester, Millbury, Westborough, Framingham, Natick, Weston and Newton, my excitement swelled to near-unbearable levels. Upon spotting the unpretentious little roadside announcement that says "Boston city limits," which leaps into view at about the same moment that the tops of the Prudential Center and the Hancock Tower become visible in the distance, I knew I'd arrived where I'd always wanted to be.

It is a strange phenomenon, this tug on the heart exerted by exotic mostly-faraway destinations—this pull that initially manifests itself in the form of pictures flashed across a television screen or people and scenes depicted on the pages of an encyclopedia, magazine or travel book. The yearning for "greener pastures," the need to escape the perimeter of a birthplace that often seems all the more confining or uninspiring with each passing year, is a natural instinct. Some people act when such an urge strikes; some don't.

As a ten-year-old whose aspirations played out to the sound of a basketball bouncing up and down on the blacktop driveway of our home, mention of the name Boston immediately evoked images of men clad in white with green trim who repeatedly ran opponents dizzy on the parquet floor of the Boston Garden. The checkered floor of "the Garden" was arguably the most famous playing surface in the entire world of sport; it alone was worth ten points toward victory, by my calculations.

The shamrock the Boston Celtics used as their team logo told me they possessed the luck of the Irish; the whippings they administered to the Philadelphia 76ers, the Chicago Bulls, the Los Angeles Lakers and the Detroit Pistons indicated to me that they didn't need a four-leaf clover to get the job done. The amalgamation of talent assembled under the roof of the ancient building on Causeway Street by the team's crusty and cagey coach—Arnold "Red" Auerbach—negated the necessity of witch doctors, magic potions, rabbit's feet or a genie in a bottle. All it took for the next morning's headlines to scream, "Celtics win!" was a long running one-handed shot pushed forward from the chest by Bob Cousy, a short shot banked off the glass and through the rim by Tommy Heinsohn or a deft block to kill an enemy rally exercised by Bill Russell.

There is no explaining how a New York kid falls head over heels under the spell of a team situated three hundred miles away (and in a state that is not his own to boot). And yet this is what happened, as I stretched out in front of the TV on Sunday afternoons to watch "the Green" parade their skills. I celebrated with all of Boston—and grew more enamored of this seemingly invincible franchise, with each victory; I cheered with Celtics fans everywhere as still another championship banner was raised to the rafters.

Eventually Larry Bird (the greatest white player ever) would come along to take the place of K.C. Jones, Bill Sharman, Frank Ramsey and Sam Jones and lead the Celtics to further glory.

The Celtics defined Boston to me long before I knew anything about the ingredients that would later emerge as equally compelling symbols of the city of "the bean and the cod."

The first of these that I encountered were Fred and Judith Phinney. Together the Phinneys headed up a newspaper company called Citizen Group Publications. Situated in a small one-story building on Harvard Street in Brookline, "CGP" was already producing three weekly tabloid newspapers (the *Brookline Citizen*, the *Allston-Brighton Item* and the *Boston Ledger*) when I arrived and would soon launch a fourth (the *Charlestown Ledger*). The *Charlestown Ledger* was created specifically to celebrate the rejuvenation of the old Navy Yard-sector of the city of Boston; Charlestown was in the midst of a total transformation, as a number of seemingly outdated brick and stone-fronted structures (all within easy walking distance of the U.S.S. Constitution) were being turned into upscale, high-priced condominiums for yuppies. Restaurants and shops were taking root on Charlestown's cobbled streets, too. In a flash, young persons who owned BMWs and Volvos and Audis were strolling the very same passageways that had formerly teemed with sailors outfitted in spit-shined black shoes and starched white caps.

It was into this environment that I was thrust: a country boy summoned to the big city to take on the enormous task of directing a small staff of eager but unpolished young reporters in the publication of newspapers that would somehow draw readers' attention away from the bigger, sassier, more deeply entrenched *Boston Globe*, *Boston Herald* and *Boston Phoenix*.

A short man with frizzy hair who possessed the buoyant personality of a traveling salesman and the brimming confidence of a professional wrestler, Fred Phinney firmly believed he could carve a niche for himself in the rough-and-tumble world of Boston journalism. Full of ambition, bluster and moxie, he was convinced nothing could stop him in his quest to garner attention. His every move gave the impression that he already owned the town. When wining and dining prospective benefactors over lunch at one of his favorite Coolidge Corner restaurants, he would pull his car to a screeching halt in a "no-parking" zone, fly through the front door, throw an arm around the hostess and say, "Hello, you beautiful doll, hook me up with a table for two, please, and we're in kind of a hurry." Upon inviting young Joe Kennedy, who was running for Congress, to Brookline for a first-ever meeting to discuss the status of Kennedy's campaign, he'd blitz his guest with all sorts of charm, assure him he would have the editorial endorsement of the CGP newspapers, vigorously shake his hand as they parted and declare, by way of mild admonishment, as if they'd been bosom buddies since childhood, "Don't be a stranger now." When then-Boston Mayor Ray Flynn or some other politician staged a fundraising event at the brand-new Embassy Suites hotel overlooking Storrow Drive, Fred would breeze into the room bearing the regal presence of an ambassador to a foreign country and immediately careen from one person to the next—gushing flatteries.

And so it went. There were expensive dinners at the Stockyard, a steakhouse alongside the Mass Pike in Allston. There was an evening bash at Boston University in recognition of Author Elie Wiesel thrown on Wiesel's behalf by BU President John Silber. There was the glitzy launch of the new Four Seasons hotel, a night at the Hampshire House on Beacon Street as a toast to the one hundredth airing of the popular television show Cheers and the dedication of a park along the water-front in tribute to Rose Kennedy. Attendance was expected at these events. It was Fred Phinney's way of letting the right people know that Citizen Group Publications was "a player."

For a little while the CGP newspapers did make something of an imprint on the local consciousness. By concentrating with the attentive-ness of a chess master on stories involving volatile neighborhood issues, Citizen Group Publications developed a reputation as a watchdog with its ear attentively affixed to the ground. Fleshy articles about the uneasy relationship that existed between Boston University and residents who lived in the vicinity of the school's sprawling Commonwealth Avenue campus became commonplace on the pages of the *Allston-Brighton Item* and the *Brookline Citizen* as BU gobbled up more and more property to house its burgeoning student population. Stories about the uproar caused by plans to transform Brookline Village from a relatively quiet governmental outpost into a magnet for shoppers with the infusion of a batch of retail stores generated screaming headlines and powerful opinions pro and con in the *Brookline Citizen*.

Stories about crime in the Fenway, about schemes for condos in the South End, about blueprints for expansion boldly laid out by St. Elizabeth's Hospital, about the nasty war of words that developed between candidates vying for seats on the Boston City Council and about Boston College's intentions to enlarge Alumni Stadium touched the nerves of residents of the city and its environs who were concerned about quality of life. Our outgunned but young and hungry news staff at Citizen Group Publications took full advantage. We worked every angle, pumped every source, quoted every principal. Week after week as CGP's newspapers rolled off the press, some new battle royal dominated the front page. In his office, with the sleeves of his Brooks Brothers shirt rolled up and his red cheeks aglow, Fred Phinney reveled in the stir Citizen Group Publications was causing. In his unbridled desire to become the next Steve Mindich or Pat Purcell of the Boston-area publishing world, he would plot his next move, concoct his next journalistic escapade and mull the opportunities available to him to ruffle his next feather.

That Citizen Group Publications was essentially a fly-by-the-seat-of-your-pants operation with no viable future as a business enterprise became apparent to me early in my association with the Phinneys. No one, least of all them, knew what would happen from one day to the next. In staid Brookline—home of Jewish synagogues and Jewish bakeries and the historic Coolidge Corner movie house and the simple two-story home on Beal Street in which John F. Kennedy spent his boyhood years—Citizen Group Publications was the convulsive odd duck. All was sweetness and light when the coffee truck pulled up each morning and pleasantries were exchanged; then all hell broke loose.

I parted company with the Phinneys just over two years after meeting them. During that time, however, I came to appreciate more keenly than ever what had lured me to Boston in the first place. Unlike New York City, the very immenseness of which is continually beguiling and at the same time daunting, Boston boasts an intimacy that nurtures the soul. Boston has been described as "a walking city" because of its intricate web of cow paths-turned-roadways. It has been described as "the San Francisco of the East" because of its European-like gentility. It has been affectionately referred to by natives as "the Hub" because of its standing as both a cornerstone of the American Revolution and a mecca of culture and commerce. It has been dubbed "Beantown" because of Bostonians' fondness for a food that has been a staple of the dinner table for generations.

"Boston" is really a much larger entity than its immediate geographic borders would suggest; it's true that fewer than a million people live within the compact sphere that is loosely bounded by Logan International Airport to the east, the Zakim and Tobin bridges to the north, the Quincy city line to the south and Route 128 to the west. Broaden the circle for forty or so miles in three directions to include Cambridge, Somerville, Wellesley, Watertown, Lexington, Concord, Everett, Needham, Dedham, Arlington and Chelsea, etc., and "Boston" suddenly mushrooms into a sprawling metropolis. When locals talk "Boston," they are referring not just to a city made famous by the likes of Paul Revere, the hotel district, Chinatown, the Wang Center, Symphony Hall, Old North Church, the Old Town Trolley, Jimmy's Harborside, Anthony's Pier 4, Ye Olde Oyster House, the State House, First Night, the Southeast "Distressway," the Museum of Fine Arts and the Black Falcon Terminal but also to Harvard and MIT, the Salem Witch Museum—even Plymouth Rock and the Bourne Bridge.

The delights of "Boston" cannot be measured solely, then, by what can be found a short walk or cab ride from Copley Square. Take a wider arc into account and the magnetism of "Boston" glows with keener intensity.

I have watched Wade Boggs slap doubles off the Green Monster from box seats along the third-base line at Fenway Park; I have viewed jugglers and unicyclists and clowns—encircled by appreciative onlookers—perform feats of skill and hilarity for nickels and dimes and quarters and dollar bills in the sunshine of the courtyard at Quincy Market; I have attended a Make-A-Wish gala hosted by Deborah Penta of Penta Communications in a swanky room of the Ritz Carlton on the Boston Common, and heard her say to generous donors as they fork over thousands of dollars, "Thank you, thank you so much!"; I have shaken hands with Jesse Jackson at Trinity Church; I have watched humanity mass by the thousands for the starting gun of the Boston Marathon in Hopkinton, and Kenyans lope like gazelles toward the finish line on Boylston Street; I have walked portions of the Freedom Trail; I have listened to *Boston Herald* "bad-boy" columnist Howie Carr discuss his book *The Brothers Bulger* in a bookstore in Winchester at which mem-

A Patriots' Day tradition, the Boston Marathon is a runnin', rockin' good time…especially on Boylston Street near the finish line.

bers of the audience stood elbow to elbow; I have ridden the Green Line as it clatters from Cleveland Circle towards North Station; I have climbed aboard The Spirit of Boston with other members of the press for its maiden voyage through Boston Harbor; I have shared a piece of the Esplanade with lovers and muggers and thieves on the Fourth of July as Keith Lockhart and the Boston Pops raise the roof of the Hatch Shell with booming brass and strings while fireworks explode overhead, lighting up the Charles River and the boats bobbing in the darkness there; I have strolled the narrow streets of the North End in search of the perfect plate of lasagna and a cannoli that leaves the tongue yearning for a second helping; I have licked an ice-cream cone on Newbury Street, shopped at Chestnut Hill, sat in rapt attention as the Pittsburgh Symphony Orchestra entertained on the opening night of the spectacular Great Woods performing-arts theater (now the Tweeter Center) in Mansfield, studied the movements of Ty Law and Troy Brown and Tom Brady during a New England Patriots' pre-season game at Gillette Stadium in Foxborough, stood in the hall of flags at the JFK Library on the edge of Dorchester Bay and laughed uproariously at the antics of Joe Martelle and the late Andy Moes of "The Joe & Andy Family" on WROR 98.5 FM mornings between 5:30 and 9:00.

Boston is small enough to wrap your arms around, and big enough to be "big league" all the way.

It is not only "Dirty Water" that The Standells sang of but a popular mayor whose nickname is "Mumbles" (Tom Menino), a talk-show host who died of complications from AIDS (the endearing David Brudnoy), a public works project that became the centerpiece for NBC-TV's "the fleecing of America" (the Big Dig), impressive films (Blown Away and The Departed) and a tunnel named after a Hall of Famer (Ted Williams).

It is truly "my home," even when I'm not there.

Early arrivals for an old-fashioned sock hop featuring the Worcester band Cathy's Clown at the Leicester Town Hall on June 10th, 2006 included Craig Swindell, in boots, leather and beret, and Pastor Nancy Milton, in a poodle skirt (both representing the host Leicester Federated Church), and Peter Morgan who appeared with his 1946 Ford Super Deluxe convertible. Morgan and his wife, Jerry, tour New England in the car, which, he says, "Reminds us of a car we had around the time we got married." Before long, all were on the dance floor, and it was 1958 again!

XX. SOCK HOPS

"Well, you can swing it, you can groove it
You can really start to move it at the hop
Where the jockey is the smoothest
And the music is the coolest at the hop
All the cats and chicks
can get their kicks at the hop
Let's go!"

"At The Hop"
Danny and The Juniors
ABC-Paramount Records, 1957

D uring an interview with Paul Lauzon of Worcester's WCUW (91.3 FM) that occurred by telephone on June 22, 2006, Tony Testa of The Duprees made the point that no "generational music" has had the "staying power" of the Rock & Roll that was produced in the late 1950s and early 1960s. This is not a far-fetched claim but a grounded truth: in dance clubs, at weddings and other social gatherings, in homes and as background for television shows and television commercials (TV's "Wonder Years" and "American Dreams" come to mind), people of all ages and persuasions continue to turn to the sounds that came out of "Rock & Roll's greatest decade" (1956-1966) for guidance, inspiration and solace. The same cannot be said of the music produced by "the cowboys" (Gene Autry, Roy Rogers, et al), the big bands (Benny Goodman, Glenn Miller), Country & Western's giants of yesteryear (Bob Wills, Roy Acuff) or "the crooners" (Bing Crosby, Johnny Mathis, Tony Bennett, Nat King Cole, Judy Garland)—enduring as their contributions to the music scene may be. Even the hallowed voice of Frank

Sinatra is mostly limited to Italian restaurants these days. Typical of early Rock's songs that still echo across the landscape is "At The Hop" by Danny and The Juniors; "a monumental hit" on five continents upon being released, "At The Hop" remains one of the top twenty-five or so recordings of all time according to Billboard *magazine. It propelled the Philadelphia group Danny and The Juniors (Frank Maffei, Danny Rapp, Joe Terranova and Dave White) to instant stardom; it also put the band on the road with such legends as Fats Domino, Chuck Berry, Buddy Holly, Jerry Lee Lewis and The Platters as part of the famous "Alan Freed Big Beat Show," and established them as one of Rock's best-known acts. This might not have happened at all if Danny and The Juniors had not lip-synced "At The Hop" on Dick Clark's "American Bandstand" as a last-minute stand-in for Little Anthony and The Imperials in the Fall of 1957. The song was an immediate sensation, and quickly went to No. 1. It has remained a favorite ever since.*

Once, homes had black and white television sets for the first time. Once, there were jukeboxes everywhere. Once, movies did not have to carry the stigma of a "rating." Once, there were 45 RPM records and these were collected like baseball cards. Once, there were sock hops.

If the America of the 1950s was not a better place, it was at least a simpler place: less complicated; less noisy; less demanding; less obtrusive; less busy.

People born in the 1940s, including those who belong to what is now known as the "Baby Boomer" generation, love to turn the clock back to a quieter time—a time when there were fewer choices, fewer distractions, fewer obligations, fewer responsibilities.

It was a golden moment in the history of the nation.

Most of the sports in which I engaged as a boy growing up in a cozy community nestled along the flood-prone Susquehanna River in upstate New York did not occur in an organized setting but on the makeshift sandlots that were carved out of otherwise unused land in different neighborhoods sprinkled throughout the area. "Games" materialized on the spur of the moment as the spirit moved. They were played on the grounds of the local elementary school, in someone's backyard, in another person's driveway, in the street.

This pattern replicated itself in big cities and small towns across the country.

Equipment usually consisted of just the essentials: a football; a bat and baseball and mitt; a basketball. No one felt the need to purchase or wear pads or helmets or jocks or cleats. It was a "come-as-you-are" party with no uniforms to be donned, no parents yelling from the bleachers, no coaches shouting instructions from the bench, no adult keeping score in the press box and no clock ticking off the minutes and seconds.

It was as good as it gets. Richard Bach's *Jonathan Livingston Seagull* could not have been in a more euphoric state of mind in his own idyllic world, soaring, diving and searching "far out at sea, hungry, happy, learning."

The other parts of a young person's life were every bit as rewarding. "Hamburger joints" may have lacked a set of golden arches that could be seen from half a mile away, but they exuded charm and character. They weren't found near the exit ramps of major highways and along highly traveled main roads but in the heart of the business district next door to the barbershop or the hardware store or inside Woolworth's in downtowns that pulsated with excitement. The grill was not hidden from view; it was always right in front of you. As a result, the sizzle of frying meat was a constant. So too was the chatter; conversation was as integral an ingredient as the menu, the salt and pepper shakers and the bottle of ketchup sitting on the counter. You knew the owner or the waiters and waitresses and other customers by name and the dialogue back and forth was as open and animated as if it were occurring in the living room of the family home. In such an atmosphere of candor and congeniality, there were few secrets.

A male teenager's existence in those days would have been full but not overwhelming: church on Sunday and then grandma's house for dinner; school and sports; out with friends to the soda shop or a movie on Friday night; sleep late on Saturday and then off on the bicycle to a pre-arranged meeting spot for a choosing of sides among cronies and the start of "the game." "The game" dragged on for hours; intermittently there would be moments of respite: an opportunity to lie on the grass and study the clouds, or to sit on the court, cross-legged, and talk about girls. No cell phones, no computers, no adults peering around the corner to make sure that everything was on the up and up. After that, as dusk fell, came the ride home. It didn't matter if it was eight or nine o'clock in the evening: the door was always unlocked. There was little chance of encountering trouble along the way and no likelihood of anyone filing a missing-person's report if you violated "curfew."

The discovery during this period of a new rage called "Rock & Roll" sweetened the circumstances considerably; it was like sinking my teeth into one of my mom's cinnamon buns or chocolate éclairs and realizing that she had poured her usual generous helping of sugar into the batter.

With Rock & Roll came not only 45 RPM records like Buddy Holly's "That'll Be the Day" and The Four Lads' "Standing On the Corner" and Bobby Day's "Rockin' Robin" and Elvis Presley's "Hound Dog" but "sock hops."

Sock hops (presumably so named because the principals of the high schools where these happenings were typically held asked kids to remove their shoes so they wouldn't scruff up the gymnasium floor) were God's way of saying to 50s teenagers, "Just when you thought life couldn't get any better, I give you this!"

For those of us living in Endicott, New York, sock hops represented a chance to venture beyond the small world we knew to a place a little farther removed from our parents' purview. For my generation, that meant a recreation hall in the next town to the east—Johnson City. There we saw an early Rock & Roll star face to face for the first time. His name: Dion DiMucci. The group: Dion and the Belmonts.

At sock hops, we could get out from under our parents' thumb for a little while and let our hair down; hang with friends, smoke, talk jive, flirt, be cool.

It is not surprising that when members of the Leicester Federated Church in Leicester, Massachusetts decided in the winter of 2006 to stage a fundraising event, they chose a sock hop as the theme; or that they picked the gymnasium of the Leicester Town Hall as the venue. The site was a perfect fit.

"I went to high school in this building," Cindy LaPointe said, between dances. "We had sock hops here every Friday night. It was all there was to do. My mother wouldn't let me go to the drive-in!"

The atmosphere for the sock hop, which was held on an unusually blustery and raw June night, reminded those who participated of the way it was in the late 1950s when artists like Dion and the Belmonts, The Champs, Carl Perkins, The Chordettes, The Silhouettes and The Dell Vikings came along to literally blow the doors off.

All of the ingredients of a genuine old-fashioned sock hop were present. Peter Morgan's 1946 Ford convertible was on display outside the hall (his daughter Gail later showed up with a 1931 Ford); "This automobile reminds us of a car we had around the time we got married," Morgan said. "On a rainy night, we had to put an umbrella up to stay dry." Today, Morgan tours New England in his '46 Ford. He rarely encounters sock hops, though!

Inside the building, Craig Swindell and the Rev. Nancy Milton—representing the Leicester Federated Church—greeted participants as they arrived. Swindell and Pastor Milton were dressed for the occasion. Swindell could have been mistaken for "Danny" from Grease with his outfit, which consisted of a black beret, black leather jacket, black jeans and leather boots. Pastor Milton was attired in a poodle skirt. They made the ideal "couple."

The premises were straight out of the '50s: a poster mounted on a door at the entrance to the building invited one and all to "ROCK AROUND THE CLOCK;" replica 45 records hung from balloons that

It was "Rock Around the Clock" time from the opening strains of songs performed by the group Cathy's Clown at an old-fashioned sock hop at the Leicester Town Hall in June of 2006.

were draped from the ceiling; giant posters of Elvis graced the walls. Shortly after seven o'clock, as advertised, a nine-piece band called Cathy's Clown took the stage. Cathy's Clown was the crowning touch. Without the group, which was made up of mostly young musicians who also play in other bands around the Central Massachusetts area, the evening would not have been nearly as good. Perhaps Ritchie Valens or Buddy Holly sprinkled magic dust on their heads from above; whatever the reason, Cathy's Clown nailed it from the instant the band performed the first number: appropriately, "At The Hop."

Debbie Arsenault's daughter Charlene functioned as keyboardist for Cathy's Clown, and her son Duncan served as a soundman for the evening. Mom was a proud organizer and spectator.

"This band played together for the first time a year ago at a special band concert and it's kind of taken off," Debbie Arsenault said.

In covering such long-ago hits as "Book of Love," "Splish Splash," "Earth Angel," "Blue Moon," "Sweet Nothings," "Chantilly Lace," "Blueberry Hill," "La Bamba," "Johnny B. Goode," "Cupid," "No Particular Place To Go," "Great Balls of Fire" and "It's My Party" with gusto and exactly the right touch, Cathy's Clown provided those in attendance with every reason to jump onto the dance floor. "Jump" may be the wrong word, because most members of the crowd don't hop or skip much anymore; but from the old folks who line danced at one side of the gym to the middle-aged types who jitterbugged and twisted and waltzed to the twenty-something's who bumped and ground and shook and stomped, there was hardly a person present who sat still.

With Cathy's Clown hitting all the notes and with the insertion of a dance contest to the strains of Dion's "Runaround Sue," a hula-hoop contest and a Best 50s Costume competition, the sock hop never missed a beat.

To their eternal disadvantage, today's kids have nothing that remotely resembles sock hops for entertainment. Candy cigarettes, white-buck shoes, penny loafers, souped-up cars, nights at the drive-in, cherry cokes and jukeboxes are all largely a thing of the past. Worse, the Age of Innocence has given way to the Age of Gadgets.

It's hard to believe that their world, for all its techno babble, is a better place in which to grow up than the one I knew as a kid. The one that had, as a core ingredient, sock hops!

A visit to Busch Gardens in February of 2006 was made all the more memorable by the opportunity to see "Herman's Hermits starring Peter Noone" live on stage at Stanleyville Theater. The charisma for which Noone has been celebrated since his emergence as a childhood television star and then as lead vocalist for the original British rock band Herman's Hermits was on full display in his easy banter with an audience that included young children. At one point he told the crowd, "If you want to know how old we are, go to the website: who'sstillalive.com!" The quintessential entertainer, Noone kept onlookers enthralled for about forty-five minutes; the best treat of all came, of course, when he pulled classics from the Hermits' portfolio that anyone could identify with; among these were "Mrs. Brown You've Got a Lovely Daughter" and of course "I'm Henry VIII, I Am." Encountering "Herman's Hermits starring Peter Noone" strictly by accident is indeed an excellent time to say, as one of the band's song titles does, "I'm Into Something Good."

XXI. ROCKERS

"You shake my nerves
and you rattle my brain
Too much love drives a man insane
You broke my will, oh what a thrill
Goodness gracious great balls of fire"

"Great Balls of Fire"
Jerry Lee Lewis
Sun Records, 1957

I t is hard to describe what it was like to discover Jerry Lee Lewis at about the same time that I turned thirteen years old, in 1958. He'd only cut his first Rock & Roll record three years earlier, and had hit it big soon after with the release of "Whole Lotta Shakin' Going On" and then "Great Balls of Fire." What really caught my attention, and that of a whole generation, however, was the maniacal way he worked the piano. It was an instrument he'd mastered at a young age, growing up poor in Ferriday, Louisiana. He'd learned to play the piano while practicing with his cousins Mickey Gilley and Jimmy Lee Swaggart, and by observing the technique used by an older cousin—Carl McVoy—coupled with what he heard coming from the radio and from the confines of "the African American joint across the tracks at Haney's Big Home." It all meshed in his mind as he developed his own style; mixing R&B, Boogie Woogie, Gospel and Country, he became not only a proficient pianist but a powder keg of activity on the bench and at the keyboard. When I caught my first glimpse of him as a teenager I could not believe my eyes; he was a hellcat in constant motion, squirming, kicking, shouting, *standing and pounding away to beat the band. His stringy blond locks flew in every direction. I was immediately hooked. I didn't find out until much later that his yearning for self-expression had gotten him bounced from a Bible seminary in Wacahachie, Texas, after he stunned school administrators—and the audience—by playing "worldly" music. He was on his way! Jack Clement knew he'd found an immense new talent when he recorded Jerry Lee for the Sun label; Jerry Lee soon fell into and became a charter member of an impromptu jam group that would be dubbed "the Million Dollar Quartet"—consisting of himself, Elvis Presley, Carl Perkins and Johnny Cash. Still touring and "pumping" as of the Summer of 2006, he will forever be known to his fans as "The Killer." He does indeed knock 'em dead!*

Rock & Roll arrived with a bang and has been making a lot of noise ever since. Almost from the beginning, its greatest performers have gravitated toward a life marked by a fondness for alcohol, drugs, womanizing, personal conflict and non-conformity. Surprisingly, this has only endeared them that much more to fans, who can't seem to get enough.

Their appeal would not be nearly as universal if Rock & Rollers were known only through their music; of seeming equal importance to those who indulge them is their often unpredictable and deplorable behavior—on and off stage.

Granted, an argument could be made that Elvis Presley's candle would have burned even more brightly if he had not "gone kinky." Elvis' impact was certainly as immense as any performer could have hoped when he was at the height of his powers; the exposure he received from his record albums, radio, television, movies and live shows surpassed that garnered by any of his peers. His demise was all the worse because it was a slide played out in living color at a snail's pace as a nation watched (partly in chagrin, partly in condemnation, partly in bafflement).

And yet even so sad an unraveling as Elvis underwent has without a doubt contributed in some measure to the almost mythological stature "The King" enjoys today as the planet's most instantly recognizable personality. There are plenty of us who wish it had remained otherwise; a majority of his admirers could have done without the gaudy jumpsuits, the ballooned body, the shortness of breath and the heavily perspiring brow. Still, the transformation from the sculpted, shoulders-squared, clean-shaven, cherubic-faced Elvis of *G.I. Blues*, *Girls, Girls, Girls* or *Blue Hawaii* fame to the pathetic, forlorn, drug-ravaged Elvis in Decline that we had the misfortune of knowing in The Later Years is an integral part of who he is in our consciousness—for better or worse.

And so it has gone with what appears to be a vast majority of the people who have risen to prominence with a guitar nestled in their hands, a harmonica pressed to their lips or a microphone placed in front of their face. From Merle Haggard who sings so often and so poignantly of the time he spent in prison during an incorrigible youth—despite the fact that, as he puts it in one of his hits, "Mama Tried"—to Johnny Cash who seemed bent on drowning the misery he felt over the untimely loss of his older brother Jack in a stream of misadventures to Madonna who has shown she is not adverse to planting a suggestive, open-mouthed kiss on Britney Spears or Christina Aguilera as millions watch on MTV (or perpetrating a "mock crucifixion"), musicians have gravitated as naturally toward the risqué as they have toward classic notes, rhymes and melodies.

As was true of Jim Morrison of The Doors, Rockers appear to possess virtually a predisposition toward self-destruction. It's as if they are instructed at the outset of their careers by the gatekeeper, "You cannot enter this domain unless you sign a written agreement to do awful stuff to yourself or others."

In Jim Morrison's case, the end came at the age of thirty-seven but not before he had completed what The Grateful Dead would agree was "a long, strange trip" that began with a vision of dead Indians scattered along the highway in the desert and that subsequently also included regular dips into darkness and madness, a vast consumption of LSD and alcohol, sexual encounters with fans and fellow celebrities, accusations of indecent exposure and public profanity and a death that remains mired in mystery.

What a waste, one would think, of a mind that showed such promise. Highly intelligent, bookish and philosophical, Jim Morrison wound up believing, as William Blake put it, that "the road of excess leads to the palace of wisdom." The monikers he eventually acquired as "The Lizard King" and "Mr. Mojo Risin' " were a testament to his dogged allegiance to this way of thinking.

Today when Jim Morrison's name is mentioned the thought that immediately surfaces is not, "Wow, he gave us 'L.A. Woman' and 'Light My Fire' " but rather "isn't he that nut who's buried in Paris?"

Jim Morrison really did "Break On Through (To The Other Side)." And there he resides, physically interred—no doubt restlessly—in "The Poets' Corner" of the Pere Lachaire Cemetery, his legacy forever scarred by controversy and confusion.

The parallels between "The Life and Times of Jim Morrison" and those of Jimi Hendrix are too similar to ignore; they underscore the path to doom that so many members of the fraternity take—by choice, or inadvertently.

Hendrix succumbed at the age of twenty-seven amid the same sort of "unexplained" circumstances that claimed Morrison's life. Found dead in the basement flat of the Samarkand Hotel in London in the early-morning hours of September 18, 1970 after spending the night there with his German girlfriend Monika Dannenmann, Hendrix had been steaming toward a rendezvous with disaster in such a Titantic-like rush that no angel could have intervened on his behalf. Strung out for years on hallucinogenic drugs, he had already accumulated a dossier of incidents so bizarre that even his closest friends shook their heads in disapproval. There was the time he beat his British babe, Kathy Etchingham, in a London pub with the handset of a pay telephone in a fit of jealousy when he thought she was calling another man. There was the time he got drunk and was arrested for destroying a Stockholm hotel room. There was the time he punched Paul Caruso, a fellow musician, in the face. He also reportedly fathered two children, neither of whom he ever met or acknowledged. As if to perpetrate the aura of craziness that surrounded him, Hendrix even claimed he had a one-night stand with actress Brigitte Bardot in Paris while en route home from a sojourn in Morocco.

And so it is that Jimi Hendrix is remembered as vividly for the quirkiness that preceded his demise as he is for the Stratocaster guitar that he played so magnificently or the amazing solo improvisation of "The Star-Spangled Banner" that he rendered as the main attraction at Woodstock in August of 1969.

This gravitation toward the absurd that so often seizes the life of musicians explains why Kurt Cobain is perhaps better remembered for dying of a self-inflicted shotgun wound to the head than for helping the band Nirvana usher in the ascendancy of grunge and alternative rock in the 1990s. The very picture of innocence as a child, Cobain started acting weird shortly after his parents divorced when he was eight; as a kid, he attached a set of firecrackers to a piece of metal, placed it on his chest, and lit it. As an adult, he lived under a bridge for a while after being kicked out of his mother's house. He was arrested for vandalism and trespassing. In an attempt to deal with prolonged periods of depression and physical pain caused by chronic bronchitis and an undiagnosed stomach condition that plagued him for years, he self-medicated with heroin. Marriage (to Courtney Love) could not save him. Step by step he marched steadily toward a date with suicide.

A purported suicide note he wrote upon taking his own life at the age of twenty-seven (some people theorized that he had been murdered) compelled Kurt Cobain to quote a line from the Neil Young song "My My, Hey Hey (Out of the Blue)," which goes, "It's better to burn out than fade away."

Janis Joplin is likewise singularly recalled for her "anything-goes" lifestyle. Possessed of a powerful, distinctive voice and widely recognized for her scorching vocals, flamboyant fashion, outspokenness and sense of humor, Joplin was one of the first women to front a full-fledged Rock band. And yet the image that stands apart from all others she left is that of a washout who OD'd on heroin in a motel in Los Angeles in October of 1970.

As has so often been the case, Joplin could not break free from a dependence that began early and deepened quickly; admonitions from friends that "the two (music and drugs) aren't wedded" made no difference. The articulate, shy, sensitive girl from Port Arthur, Texas who seemed destined to surpass even the accomplishments in the sphere of Blues mustered by her childhood idols—Bessie Smith, Odetta and Leadbelly—ultimately surrendered herself to the devil. Having drifted into a habit of using alcohol and drugs (including speed) while playing coffee houses and hootenannies in small towns around the Lone Star State, she attempted to "go clean" but never succeeded in that effort. Her end came far too soon after she'd hooked up with a relatively obscure band called "Big Brother and the Holding Company" in San Francisco and personally smashed the barrier of anonymity that was keeping her back with a rendition of Big Mama Thornton's "Ball and Chain" that left listeners breathless.

Such is life in the Land of the Living Dead: Hendrix, dead at twenty-seven; Joplin, dead at twenty-seven; Cobain, dead at twenty-seven.

A startling number of notables from the world of Rock have "been there" to one degree or another in terms of flirting with disaster as they climbed the ladder to the top. What began with the unfortunate fiery deaths of Buddy Holly, Ritchie Valens and "The Big Bopper" (J. P. Richardson) in an airplane crash that was an avoidable accident has morphed into a situation in which their successors in the medium choose to operate on the very edge of a deep black hole. In their defiance of the limitations of time and space Rockers continually place themselves in great jeopardy; oddly enough, this has not lessened but rather heightened their winsomeness in the eyes of their fans. In a strange twist of fate, the reputations of individual greats (e.g., Kris

Kristofferson, Elton John, Rod Stewart, George Jones, Ray Charles, et al) and legendary groups (The Rolling Stones, The Grateful Dead, The Band, The Beatles, The Who) alike have been burnished rather than tarnished by their tawdry behavior.

Even those Rockers who have hung around for a while often carry with them the stigma of misdirection. No better example exists than Jerry Lee Lewis, who got himself nearly excommunicated from Rock & Roll and almost banned from the United States too by marrying his thirteen-year-old second cousin once-removed—Myra Gale Brown—when he was in his early twenties. I remember it as one of the most scandalous affairs ever to hit the newspapers; it ranked right up there with the Profumo incident. And yet their marriage (which didn't last) represented only a fraction of the torment Jerry Lee Lewis has had to endure during a tumultuous life; he has lost two sons, he has been plagued by alcohol and drug addiction. He even once accidentally shot his bass player, Butch Owens, in the chest.

In looking at the history of Rock & Roll's first fifty years (1956-2006), it is impossible to separate artists' music from their antics; the escapades in which they've engaged are as integral a part of who they are in the public's eye as the grooves on the vinyl records they've created. It's no surprise therefore that The Rolling Stones are as well-known for their digressions as for such celebrated hits as "Time Is on My Side," "Satisfaction," "Jumpin' Jack Flash" and "Start Me Up." Their hedonism is legendary. A 1967 drug bust at Keith Richards' home in Sussex (and the riotous aftermath of that incident) made headlines around the globe. The death of original member Brian Jones, who was found at the bottom of his swimming pool, surrounded by statues of Christopher Robin and Winnie the Pooh, typifies the notoriety that has shadowed their careers. Their near-constant flirtations with lawlessness have not hurt them one bit, however; inspired by Mick Jagger's mercurial personality, theatrical talents and astute business-management skills, they are bigger than ever. Mick Jagger was even knighted! Go figure!

This has been the typical scenario: whether it is Ricky Nelson turning away from the nice-boy image he initially projected on his parents' Ozzie and Harriett TV show, Chuck Berry being sentenced to ten years in the Intermediate Reformatory for Young Men near Jefferson, Missouri after being convicted of armed robbery as a teenager, Eric Clapton getting hooked on heroin and having affairs outside of his marriage to Pattie-Boyd Harrison, the late Warren Zevon consuming such large quantities of vodka that he was tagged with the nickname "F. Scott Fitzevon" or The Eagles' Don Henley getting arrested for possession of cocaine, Quaalude and marijuana when he was found in a hotel room with a nude sixteen-year-old prostitute who was suffering from convulsions, Rock's greatest performers' work has been magnified—and enhanced—by their outrageousness.

Society's response to the ever-steady drumbeat of discordance has not only been tolerance, but acceptance and even adoration. When it comes to our Rock & Rollers, "we" allow them leeway not because we approve of what they're doing but because we love them so much regardless of their indiscretions.

XXII. AMERICA

"This land is your land,
this land is my land
From California to the New York island;
From the redwood forest
to the Gulf Stream waters
This land was made for you and me"

"This Land Is Your Land"
Woody Guthrie
Folkways Records, 1944

*H*ow is it possible that a boy born into unpromising circumstances in a small frontier town and whose life was scarred by tragedy almost from the outset can emerge as one of the greatest songwriters America has ever produced? The answer lies in the precocious, inquisitive and perceptive nature Woodrow Wilson Guthrie exhibited from the moment he came into the world on July 14, 1912 in Okemah, Oklahoma. Stigmatized by the untimely death of his older sister Clara, the financial and physical ruin his family experienced when the Great Dust Storm struck the Great Plains and the institutionalization of his mother, Woody Guthrie nevertheless managed to achieve much before succumbing to the ravages of the same disease that killed Nora Belle Guthrie (Huntington's Chorea). He died October 3, 1967 at Creedmoor State Hospital in Queens, New York at the age of fifty-five. Along the way, Woody Guthrie joined the mass migration of Dust Bowl refugees—"Okies"—west in pursuit of a better life; penniless and hungry, he hitchhiked, rode freight trains and walked to California. This bittersweet trek instilled in him a love of traveling and the open road that would remain a

Sinatra could send shivers up and down the spine, singing "America the Beautiful" before an awe-struck crowd in Chicago; the same emotions were evoked, for me, when I ran into Bob Elliott of Southborough—with the Sudbury Company of Militia and Minutemen—and Kim Nuttale of Boston and Denise Oliver of Douglas (in period garb, left and right, respectively) during a Colonial muster on the grounds of the Willard House and Clock Museum in Grafton in October of 2006. The event featured musket and cannon firings, marching and drilling, food and crafts, and Colonial-era wares for sale. Only in "the Land of the Free!"

constant for the rest of his years. It also provided him with some of the material from which he initially captured attention and affection, through the issuance of such Dust Bowl ballads as "I Ain't Got No Home," "Blowin' Down the Road Feelin' Bad," "Talking Dust Bowl Blues," "Tom Joad" and "Hard Travelin.'" Working with such friends and collaborators as Lead Belly, Cisco Houston, Burl Ives, Pete Seeger, Will Geer, Sony Terry, Brownie McGhee, Josh White, Millard Lampell, Bess Hawes and Sis Cunningham, Guthrie became a champion of the disenfranchised, the destitute and the downtrodden. And yet for all of his brilliance as the author of political songs of protest, he was strongly patriotic. During World War II, motivated by his detestation of Fascism, he served in both the U.S. Merchant Marine and the U.S. Army. A creative whirlwind, he left us with remarkable statements (songs, paintings, drawings, prose) marked by "stinging honesty, humor and wit," drawn from his observation of the momentous events of the 20th Century. He is an American original, and a still-appreciated national treasure.

America has long been looked upon as the leader of the free world, a place where anything is possible, the same seemingly blessed ground on which Babe Ruth hit sixty home runs, Norman Rockwell painted masterpieces, Will Rogers uttered homespun commentary that was laced with sharp satirical points, Tiger Woods emerged as a golfing prodigy, Elvis Presley ushered in the Age of Rock & Roll and Bob Hope made the populace laugh and feel good. What a tragedy it would be if, having come so far, we let it slip away.

The celebration of Independence Day in Hampton Beach, New Hampshire, starts well in advance of midnight, July 3rd. This could easily be attributed to the town's reputation as "Party-Time Central, U.S.A." On any given day, a walk east from Ashworth Avenue along any of the alphabet streets that run perpendicular to the ocean reveals hundreds of empty, loosely bagged beer cans piled high against the curb.

The sight would surely bring a glow of satisfaction to the face of August Busch III or Pete Coors, were either to stumble upon them as they made their way by foot to dinner "on the strip" at McGuirk's, the Sea Crest or Guido Murphy's.

With the arrival of nightfall in Hampton Beach come the fireworks. Here again, the emphasis is on excess. Seemingly from every yard, from every bog, from every boat, from every spit of sand that can be found, fools who think they know something about the art of pyrotechnics light match to fuse. Instantly, an evening's peace is shattered by thunderclaps. In a nanosecond, the sky is transformed from black to a shower of red, orange, blue, green, purple and white. Far off in the distance to the west, umbrella-shaped plumes of color dot the horizon for miles on end, north and south—offering further mute but unmistakable acknowledgement that America's birthday is at hand.

Even before the main event began on Hampton Beach proper at 9:30 p.m. on July 4, 2006, enthusiasts had established a fortified position; their push to gain total control of Ocean Boulevard was so intense in scope that it brought to mind the daring of Lt. Gen. George S. Patton Jr. as "Old Blood and Guts" led the 3rd Army's drive across Germany that helped bring World War II to a close. As rockets flared overhead in a prelude to the actual proceedings, seven-year-old Emily Grace Caron of Northbridge, Massachusetts, could not resist the urge to let her excitement show (bubbling as it was, like a volcano ready to explode). "It's fireworks mania!" she said, as she ran in circles around the spot at which her family was encamped.

Memorial Day observances and Fourth of July flag waving, picnics and fireworks as demonstrations of the fervor Americans feel for the freedoms they enjoy notwithstanding, it is easy in these troubled times to experience a sense of dread. Perhaps, given the animosity directed towards America by those who consider us a bully, or who just plain dislike us (North Korea, the Palestinians, Iran, Syria, Lebanon), our days are numbered? Perhaps this grand and proud experiment in democracy has run its course? Maybe the republic to whose shores and borders so many immigrants have flocked for refuge and a new, more promising start is doomed to failure after all, after a glorious beginning and just a little over two hundred years in existence?

There have even been suggestions from learned quarters that divisions festering within our own walls will prove to be the nation's undoing; that "the United States" has become "the untied states:" liberal vs. conservative, "warmongers" vs. "peaceniks," proponents of "progress" vs. environmentalists, gay vs. straight, rich vs. poor, black vs. white, Red vs. Blue (some observers have alluded to the formation of a "shadow government" within Democratic circles to monitor and to undercut the roundly criticized policies of George W. Bush's administration). It is not so preposterous to assert that the equivalent of a "political Civil War" is raging, or to claim that the breach between the left and the right has become so wide as to represent a threat even greater than those posed by al-Qaida or Kim Jong Il.

There are indications too that Americans are increasingly less patriotic. In revealing the results of a poll in an article that appeared in the July/August 2006 AARP Bulletin entitled "How Patriotic Are We?" Reed Karaim reported that 57% of American adults who responded to a Bulletin survey identified themselves as "extremely" or "very" patriotic—a 15% falloff from the 72% number a Gallup Poll, conducted a year earlier, had produced.

A "generational divide" seems to be to blame, Karaim said. While Americans over age fifty continue to exhibit the most patriotic tendencies, this is less true than was the case twelve months prior, when Gallup Poll conductors tested sentiment; and those under age fifty—particularly persons age eighteen to thirty-four—are nowhere near as zealously loyal in their support of their country as they were as recently as 2005.

Reasons cited by individuals who participated in the AARP Bulletin's nationwide sampling included disillusionment caused by federal incompetence (FEMA "dropping the ball" in New Orleans in the aftermath of Hurricane Katrina, for instance) and a growing distrust of bureaucracy (a seventy-one year-old retired physician and political independent who feels the U.S. has no business meddling in Iraq's internal affairs said, "This is going to sound terrible, but I don't believe any politician is honest anymore").

Perhaps at no juncture in the nation's history since the bloodbath between the North and the South have these two barometers of public sentiment swung as markedly toward the negative: the feeling on the one hand that there are "two camps" or "two Americas"—separate and so far apart in their philosophical approach to issues involving the country's fate that they will never be reconciled—and the belief on the other that a patriotic attitude is futile in the face of such allegedly demonstrated ineptitude by those who lead.

It raises the question: if George Washington, Paul Revere, Nathan Hale, Benjamin Franklin, Patrick Henry, Abraham Lincoln, Robert E. Lee, Ulysses S. Grant, Teddy Roosevelt, Davy Crockett, Oliver Wendell Holmes or Harry S. Truman were alive today, would their judgment be that America is on the ascent—or in decline?

This fertile land with its shimmering oceans, stupendous mountains, mighty rivers, spacious canyons and lush valleys has continually been at the forefront of advances made in every field of human endeavor. America presented the world with the genius who "discovered electricity," and who invented the lightning rod and the Franklin stove, among his numerous other accomplishments, for God's sake!

Over and over Americans have used the liberty they enjoy in a capitalistic society to assert themselves; time and again they have managed to shock and awe the rest of mankind with their brainpower, their creativeness and their ingenuity.

Only in such an atmosphere, in which expression is allowed to blossom unimpeded by the suffocations of totalitarianism or the shackles of backward thinking, could so many of civilization's grandest breakthroughs have come to fruition. Only in a place where people who acknowledge the flag with a crisp and snappy salute and people who burn it in protest of "unjust" actions or policies have an equal opportunity to excel. Only in America could Barry Goldwater and Allen

Ginsburg stand shoulder-to-shoulder, one reading from his book *The Conscience of a Conservative*, the other reading from his poem "Howl."

No other nation, in so short a time, has generated a roster of giants that compares to America's. Out of its masses have come individuals who dominate in their chosen area of interest; enough such luminaries have emerged, in fact, to populate a small country, were the leader or rulers of such a state inclined to seek out "the best and the brightest" in order to "leaven the bread" to just the right texture.

Consider some of those who would fall into this category: Ansel Adams, arguably the planet's most extraordinary landscape and nature photographer; Samuel Adams, whose middle name, because of his proclivity for stirring up the wrath of the British, might have been "Agitator;" Neil Armstrong, who could write in his resume, if he had wanted to, "I was the first man to walk on the moon;" Henry Ford, who turned the automotive world on its head while simultaneously revolutionizing life in America with the introduction of first the Model T, in 1908, and then, a mere five years later, the assembly line; the Wright Brothers, who in December of 1903, in Kitty Hawk, North Carolina, performed the seemingly impossible by going airborne in a "flying machine;" Charles A. Lindbergh, the first person to fly nonstop across the Atlantic from New York to Paris (in 1927, in a craft he christened The Spirit of St. Louis); Gen. Douglas MacArthur, who said, "I shall return," and did, by landing in the Philippines in 1944 and overseeing the surrender of Japan, which took place aboard the battleship Missouri; Annie Oakley, who as a member of "Buffalo Bill" Cody's Wild West Show delighted and stupefied audiences with her tricks of marksmanship (she could shoot cigarettes from her husband's lips, and pepper a playing card, tossed into the air, with holes before it hit the ground); Walt Disney, without whom we would never have seen the likes of Mickey Mouse, Donald Duck or Snow White and the Seven Dwarfs (the first feature-length cartoon movie); Robert Peary, the first living being to reach the North Pole (on April 6, 1909); Betsy Ross, who crafted the first American flag; Jim Thorpe, of Indian ancestry, "the greatest athlete in the world" as so pronounced by Sweden's King Gustav V after winning gold medals in both the decathlon and pentathlon in the 1912 Olympic Games; Louis Armstrong, the esteemed "Satchmo," "the world's greatest trumpeter" and pioneer of "scat" singing; Jesse Owens, who by winning four gold medals in the 1936 Olympic Games in Berlin made a public mockery of German dictator Adolf Hitler's theories of an Aryan "master race;" and Jackie Robinson, who broke major-league baseball's color barrier when he opened the season at first base for the Brooklyn Dodgers at Ebbets Field in 1947 (to a chorus of catcalls and barbs and derision), and then quickly materialized into the sport's most electrifying player.

The real danger for America in 2007 does not come from distant drumbeats of hostility but from within. Radicals and terrorists operating out of bunkers and caves and "safe houses" in Kabul or Baghdad or Beirut are not the enemy that is going to cause our demise. If America falls, it will be because our will has been weakened by inner conflict to such an extent that we no longer have the backbone to say, with a spring in our step and fire in our eyes, "Bring it on!"

America has always derived its strength from common folk who answered the call to action in times of crisis. People like "Light-Horse Harry" Lee (father of Gen. Robert E. Lee), who abandoned plans to pursue a career in law at the outbreak of the Revolution and went on to become one of the fledging nation's most respected cavalry officers (he took part in the victorious siege at Yorktown that effectively ended the Revolution, for instance). He later served three terms as governor of Virginia. "Light-Horse Harry" was never reluctant to come to the aid of his country, regardless of what such sacrifice would cost him; when his friend George Washington asked him to help in putting down the Whiskey Rebellion of 1794, he complied.

He also gave his homeland the most famous eulogy ever spoken on American soil, when he said of his friend George Washington in an address delivered in Philadelphia upon the latter's death, "First in war, first in peace, and first in the hearts of his countrymen."

Sam Houston demonstrated similar allegiance. Largely unschooled growing up in Virginia and Tennessee, he moved into the woods at a young age and lived among the Cherokee Indians for several years. Despite these humble beginnings, Sam Houston emerged as a pre-eminent soldier and public official; he played a distinguished and prominent part in the birth of the Republic of Texas, and long advocated for equitable treatment of the American Indian. He was staunchly "pro-Union."

It is only when "average American" men and women like "Light-Horse Harry" Lee, Sam Houston and the strong-willed Clara Barton (founder of the American Red Cross) are no longer willing to heed the summons to duty that America's resolve to defend its way of life will be broken. And that won't happen unless Americans become convinced that the cause for which so many of their forebears gave their property, their loved ones and even their very lives is no longer worth the effort.

Retired U.S. Army Officer, military expert, essayist and novelist Ralph Peters (his latest book as of 2006 was *Never Quit The Fight*) has said that, when the chips are on the line, small-town America "will always do the right thing;" that the integrity, wisdom, loyalty and courage of the middle class can be counted on to carry the country through any crisis.

This has proven to be true; the veracity of Ralph Peters' argument has been repeatedly ratified at pivotal moments in our history: when the abolition of slavery tore the country asunder, during the dark days of the Great Depression, in the aftermath of Pearl Harbor, in the wake of the assassinations of the Sixties, in the face of the scourge of Watergate and in the soul-searching hours following 9/11.

Only if "one nation, under God" becomes "two, separate and plagued by irreconcilable differences," will the most powerful country on earth wither and die.

Upon meeting Kenny Rogers at the South Shore Music Circus in Cohasset in August of 2006, my wife said to him, "I just want you to know that all three of our children are Kenny Rogers fans because I have been playing your music for them since they were young." Pausing for a second to ponder that comment, Kenny replied, "That's child abuse!" In the sterling performance that followed, Kenny leavened a mix of old and new material with a jocular approach that tickled the funny bone. During audience-participation moments, he chided the crowd for singing off-key. He drew appreciative laughter when he told the story of "Sam and Joe," who became lifelong buddies through a mutual love of baseball. In old age, Kenny related, "Joe asked, 'Sam, do you think there is baseball in heaven?' " "I don't know," Sam answered, "but if I go first, I'll find out for you." Standing over Sam's casket a short while later, Joe heard a "Pssst!" "Sam, is that you?" he asked. "Yes, it's me, Joe," Sam said. "I have good news and bad news. The good news is, there IS baseball in heaven. The bad news is, you're pitching Tuesday!" Throughout the show, Kenny worked hard to win over a spectator named "Terry," who, at the outset, acknowledged that, like most men in the amphitheater, he wasn't particularly interested in being there. After running through a strong repertoire and just before singing "Lady" to close the show, Kenny tossed Terry a Kenny Rogers T-shirt. "Put it on," he instructed. Then, turning to the rest of those present, he said, "Follow Terry to the parking lot. If he takes the shirt off before he gets to his car, beat the hell out of him!"

XXIII. Risk

"You got to know when to hold 'em,
know when to fold em.
Know when to walk away
and know when to run.
You never count your money
when you're sittin at the table.
There'll be time enough for countin
When the dealins done."

"The Gambler"
Kenny Rogers
United Artists, 1978

It's laughable that Rolling Stone *magazine once dubbed Kenny Rogers* "the overweight lightweight." *The same man that* Rolling Stone *dismissed as practically irrelevant is the only singer ever to chart a record in each of six consecutive decades; as of the Summer of 2006 he had recorded fifty-one Top 20 songs (including twenty-two No. 1's) and sold something like one hundred five million albums. The most recent of these as of 2006, "Water & Bridges," illustrates once again the resiliency of his voice and the power of his message. Overcoming adversity and proving the skeptics wrong has been one of Kenny Rogers' fortes since he was a kid growing up poor in a large family in Houston. Yet from the time he first began performing with a high school Doo Wop/Rockabilly group called The Scholars, he was destined for greatness. Success didn't come immediately; although he initially gained positive notice with The New Christy Minstrels and The First Edition (remember "Just Dropped In/To See What Condition My Condition Was In?"), it wasn't until Kenny Rogers went solo and effected "crossover" appeal between Country and Pop that he hit his stride. Famous for his gravelly-voiced renditions of such hits as "Lucille," "Daytime Friends," "Rueben James," "Ruby, Don't Take Your Love to Town" and "Coward of the County," he has long since proven himself as an entertainer of the highest caliber and in a number of other ways: as an actor in films and on television, as a photographer, as a restaurateur, as a rancher, as a philanthropist. Seeing him on stage in concert provides the only evidence necessary to assert that he has earned the acclaim he is accorded by thousands of fans around the world. That he's loved is apparent in the liberties he can take with audiences that pour out their affection for him; at the South Shore Music Circus in Cohasset, Massachusetts in the Summer of 2006, after one particularly woeful sing-along effort on the part of those in attendance, he chided them by saying, "You're the worst group I've ever heard. They weren't this bad in Quebec, Canada, and they don't even speak English!"*

> **Every trip to the roulette wheel, every investment in the stock market, every walk through a rough neighborhood, every trip to the operating room and every start in the Indianapolis 500 is tinged with the prospect of tragedy. That is what makes risk so intriguing—and so potentially life-affirming.**

Accepting as a given that life is a game of chance, the question becomes, is it better to shelter oneself from any activity or endeavor that involves the slightest element of risk; or to throw caution to the wind?

There are in society those for whom danger is such a terrible prospect that they take extreme measures to maintain an environment that is devoid of outside threats. Some even do so after previously demonstrating a thirst for going beyond the norm that is marked by a decided disregard for their own fate. Howard Hughes fits into this category; the aviator who as a dashing young man harbored not a shred of apprehension about flight even though he knew it was fraught with uncertainties turned into the recluse whose every move was reflective of the paranoia he felt about suffering contamination at the hands of his fellow human beings. Bravado ultimately gave way to fear and suspicion; Howard Hughes the Conqueror evolved into Howard Hughes the Coward: a shockingly less desirable person…indeed, an abomination.

To live abundantly, one must be willing to gamble. Inherent in this compulsion is an understanding that risk carries not only the prospect of tremendous reward but also the possibility of severe calamity. Steve Irwin—"the Crocodile Hunter"—knew this long before he suffered a fatal encounter with a stingray on September 4, 2006. The barb that pierced his chest and killed him at the age of forty-four ended forever Steve Irwin's special role as an environmentalist and a "wildlife warrior," but it did not diminish his stature in the eyes of the world. Instead his fame rose.

Had he chosen to work in an unobtrusive manner as a quiet, dispassionate zookeeper or animal attendant, keeping mostly out of public view, Irwin probably would have survived to see his children grow and to tell stories to his grandkids. His contributions to the profession he pursued would have been just as appreciated, albeit on a reduced scale. He elected to follow a different path. By placing himself in front of millions through the medium known as television, by letting his natural exuberance rise to the surface and by engaging deadly creatures face-to-face with no protection against harm except his own intuitions and skills, he developed a huge following. Irwin devotees recognized that this was not an act; Steve Irwin's approach was genuine and sincere.

Risk was ever-present in situations he encountered. As Actor Kevin Costner noted during a memorial service for Irwin at the Australia Zoo that drew a throng of five thousand people, Irwin "put himself out there." He was fearless, Costner said. "He let us see who he was. That is being brave in today's society."

A willingness to accept risk is an admirable trait even when the outcome is opposite that which is envisioned. It does not matter whether the risk is taken from the muddy trenches of a foxhole on the battlefield, on the back of a horse in a polo match, over a big burnished table in a corporate boardroom, amid the shifty looks and unnerving silence that are to be found among players involved in a high-stakes hand of poker, in the suddenly sweltering heat and tumult of an accident or crisis scene, during the slow, painful, exhausting ascent of a mighty mountain or the cold, debilitating seemingly never-ending solo swim of the English Channel. There is in all worthy endeavor the existence of risk; the person who strives for attainment, knowing full well that the result could be failure—or worse—deserves to be held in greater esteem that the person who is afraid to reach higher or farther.

That risk often involves spur-of-the-moment decisions upon which an entire verdict hinges only makes its implications that much more severe. The circumstances in which the risk taker is placed at such forks in the road can vary; in one case they could be pivotal enough to mean life or death, in another they might be simply trying enough to mean the gain or loss of a large amount of money. Either way, there is not much time to react when such flashpoints occur; a split-second judgment must be made: go for it, or stand down.

An example: God must have received with comforting arms and soothing words of commendation the forty-six year-old Russian man who apparently without the hint of reluctance gave himself up to save a young girl on a slippery mountain slope in Utah in September of 2006. The child, just three, had wandered off the trail leading from Timpanogos Cave—about forty miles southeast of Salt Lake City. Seeing that she was in danger of sliding away, he grabbed for her. The man plummeted two hundred feet to his death; the child fell a shorter distance but escaped with injuries. Who would have the audacity to suggest anything but that the chance this man took (on behalf of a total stranger, no less) should result in his assignment to a bed of roses—rather than the application of a crown of thorns—as he drifted off to meet his Maker?

Everyday situations like these create sudden risk; how this risk is handled is what separates the strong from the weak. When with time running out during an appearance on the television game show "Jeopardy," "Nick" clicked on an opportunity to turn the $14,000 he had accrued into $28,000 and thus far surpass the $18,000 "Sara" had totaled to that point, he did not hesitate. "Let's make it a true daily double," Nick told Alex Trebek in announcing how much he would be wagering. Unable to answer the question, he lost everything. But by risking it all in a last-ditch attempt to snatch victory from defeat, Nick gained the respect of Sara and of everyone else who witnessed his ploy. Such intrepidness is the mark of the kind of risk taker who understands that the real reward is in trying.

Along with their A, B, C's, their arithmetic, their spelling and their cursive, children learn early the importance that is attached to risk. With the shout of "dare you, double dare you!" from a comrade, they are challenged to try and tiptoe across the rocks that protrude from a bubbling, raging, rain-swollen creek in an attempt to get to the other side without getting wet, or to scale a high chain-link fence that is guarded by a vicious Doberman pinscher in an effort to retrieve a ball that has gone astray without suffering a flesh-tearing bite. The mettle they show when confronted with such calls to action, as dubious witnesses look on, goes a long way toward establishing whether they are viewed as leaders or followers, as gamers or goats, as giants or dwarfs.

This process does not change with age; risks do not go away. They just take on a different composition. At two or twenty, at eighteen or eighty, there are choices to be made that test a person's grit. The courageous move forward, undeterred by the fate that awaits them; the timid step back, afraid that they are not up to the task.

When it comes to risk, the ancient saying, "It is better to have tried and failed than not to have tried at all" rings true. Throughout history, risk takers have shared a confidence that no gulf is too wide, no problem too complex and no proposal too far-fetched. The assuredness that marked the exploits of Harry Houdini when he held his breath under water for minutes on end while wriggling loose from the chains that bound his hands and feet bears a striking resemblance to the cockiness

"Lefty" Phil Mickelson demonstrates when he coolly yanks a two-iron from his bag for a two hundred thirty-yard shot over a lagoon with the golf tournament on the line. Mickelson, in the tradition of a Houdini, is not swayed by the thought that he could end up "drowned" and see thousands of dollars—or a win—slip from his grasp.

The respect risk takers earn by pushing all of their chips to the center of the table in a chancy bid for supremacy is fully deserved. For them, the ultimate prize is not success or failure but having tasted the sweet juices that are generated by taking a risk in the first place.

XXIV. First Daughters

"Mornin', just another day
Happy people pass my way
Lookin' in their eyes
I see a memory
I never realized
How happy you made me, oh Mandy"

"Mandy"
Barry Manilow
Bell/Arista Records, 1974

*B*arry Manilow is the very definition of suave; there are no rough edges, only a smoothness of the sort that is found in a piece of silk. It is hard to believe, given all that he has accomplished as a crooner in the style of Frank Sinatra and Johnny Mathis—indeed as a performer, composer, arranger and producer who has emerged as the greatest living entertainer on earth—that he once had to work in the mailroom at CBS to pay his way through the New York College of Music and Julliard. Almost from the moment he took up the accordion (and the piano, which he learned to play on an instrument owned by a neighbor in Brooklyn, where he grew up), Barry Manilow had a hunch that he would be making music his career. He has risen to the top of his profession in a fashion few others can say they have even remotely approached: not only are there the record sales in excess of sixty-five million as of early 2006 and the more than forty albums to consider, there are the added dimensions of television, film and Broadway credits, a Grammy award, the mentoring he provided to budding artists along the way (Bette Midler comes to mind), an autobiography (Sweet Life:*

The essence of what it means to be good to the core (the exact opposite of George Thurgood's "Bad To The Bone") is wrapped up in the glow and the smile that typically adorn the face of our beloved eldest daughter Amanda, center (pictured with her brother, Daniel, and sister, Caroline). No one can explain where such grace, thoughtfulness for others and acceptance of what trials and tribulations fall on her doorstep come from; we are left, instead, to ponder the unlikelihood of such an occurrence...and to count our blessings for her uplifting presence in our lives.

Adventures on the Way to Paradise) *and charitable projects (the Manilow Fund for Health and Hope, to name one). His star has occupied a prominent place in the musical galaxy for many years; his "In the Round World Tour" of 1981-82 set box office and building-attendance records, for instance. His appearances in the U.K. back then kicked off with five sold-out shows at Royal Albert Hall. When he arrived in London, he was met at Heathrow Airport by a deluge of fans; they had slugged their way through one of the worst storms in English history to see him, prompting the British Daily Mail to describe the scene as "a fervor scarcely matched since the heyday of Elvis Presley and The Beatles" and for headlines in newspapers in Britain to blare: "Manilow Mania." His song "Copacabana" (made forever memorable by the opening line, "Her name was Lola...") spawned a musical. Still today, with the release of his album "The Greatest Songs of The Fifties," ("Venus," "Love Is A Many Splendored Thing," "Unchained Melody") he commands due attention. Which is as it should be, for the passion prevails.*

The arrival of the eldest of the offspring provokes the initial stirrings of a paternal bliss that intensifies with each subsequent trip to the delivery room. With the emergence of "the first" springs a desire to cuddle and caress and coach and cheer and console that cannot be contained: not even Zeus, effecting the chaining of Prometheus to a rock, could stop a father—accorded a blessing of such magnitude—from unshackling himself in a sudden burst of might in order to provide shelter and sustenance to one so seemingly dependent on the boost he can offer. From this crucible is born a love that grows with the passing of the years. Always, regardless of what intervenes as the days melt away, there is the image, and the warm thoughts, of "Mandy."

A man's heart is smitten with the birth of a first child; when Fate decrees that this infant should be a girl, it is as if Creation itself has been upstaged: the grandeur of Heaven and Earth pale in comparison. No weight can shatter the euphoria a father feels upon stepping forth from the silence to cradle in his arms a daughter; no burden can squash the hope that swells in his chest as he contemplates the joy she will bring to his days and nights.

It is a sight rare as an eclipse of the sun to watch this babe, so small and seemingly helpless at the outset, begin the journey—fraught as it is with hidden traps and snares—into adolescence. There is the wonder that comes with seeing her take the early toddling steps from footstool to sofa. There is the relief that floods the body in knowing that the humiliations to which she is being subjected in the classroom and on the playground—an inevitable part of childhood—will not break her will (although the tears she sheds at the time will crush your own). There is the exhilaration that is experienced when the rebelliousness of her teenage years gives way, at last, to acceptance and—after that—to maturity. There is the anxiousness that accompanies the courtship period; Suitor F is deemed every bit as defective, in a father's eyes, as Suitor A until, finally, the realization dawns that greater significance needs to be attached to the affection the single most deserving (and persistent) pursuer applies to the quest.

There is, when this process has reached its definitive stage, and "daddy's little girl" has turned into a woman who radiates beauty from head to toe and has married and given life to her own children, the impulse to take flight, in the manner of eagles, with wings outstretched, and to proclaim on high the glorious news: "I am singularly blessed!"

No father is more fortunate than the one whose daughter is additionally endowed with a goodness that is absolute; an angel whose instincts are so inclined toward compassion and generosity as to leave all who are touched by them in wonder. Who cries hard, laughs long and lives as if tomorrow will never come.

It behooves a man presented with such a precious package to nurture, rather than stifle, her ascent; and to note, when she has fulfilled her destiny and surpassed his every expectation for her—that magic has truly been at work.

It is important for a man honored in this manner to gather humanity together and say, with celebration infusing every fiber of his being: "This is my daughter, lovely as the oceans are vast, gracious as the sky is infinite. Isn't she a sight to behold?"

"The Avenue" (Washington Avenue) in Endicott, New York, circa 1954. Trolley tracks, subsequently removed, still lined the street at that time, and angled parking—eliminated many years later—was still in evidence too. Endicott Johnson and IBM workers from nearby factories, high school students who occupied classrooms that were within walking distance, village employees, homemakers and others spilled onto The Avenue by the hundreds at lunchtime in search of a variety of goods and services. It was possible, on The Avenue, to pas a gas bill, buy a bracelet or pair of shoes, get a window screen repaired, deposit or withdraw money from a checking or savings account, obtain flowers for a special occasion, eat an éclair or watch a movie. The heyday of The Avenue, like that of the village itself, lasted for far too short a time.

XXV. Hometowns

"The old home town looks the same,
As I step down from the train,
And there to meet me is my mama
and papa
Down the road I look and there
runs Mary
Hair of gold and lips like cherries
It's good to touch the green, green
grass of home"

"Green, Green Grass Of Home"
Joan Baez
Vanguard Records, 1969

Although many view Joan Baez's career as still intertwined with that of Bob Dylan's, even though they went their separate ways—professionally—years ago, this is hardly the case. It's true that Baez continues to pay homage to the affection she and Dylan shared when they were twenty-something folk singers making social and political statements in Greenwich Village clubs and coffeehouses by regularly including Dylan standards in shows she performs today at the age of sixty-six. "Ring Them Bells," "Masters of War," "Blowin' In The Wind," "A Hard Rain's A-Gonna Fall," "It's All Over Now, Baby Blue" and "The Times They Are A'Changing" are typical examples (a famous photograph of Baez and Dylan sitting side by side as musicians at the March on Washington in 1963 is further evidence of the feelings they had for each other—starting out). And yet the body of work that Joan Baez has produced is colossal in its own right, and continues to evolve and mature as the years pass. Her distinctive soprano voice, which lilts over the land like a soft summer breeze, is one of the best in the business. Her repertoire, which is extensive, is a testament to her lifelong devotion to nonviolence. Baez's commitment to civil rights and tolerance is genuine, and deep-rooted. It can be traced all the way back to her youth, growing up in New York State and California; as the daughter of a Mexican-born father and a mother who was of Scottish and English descent, she was subjected to her share of insults and discrimination. Early on, as a result, she developed a keen interest in causes, and has been an outspoken advocate for justice ever since. Indeed, no better candidate for the Nobel Peace Prize could be found! Meanwhile, she continues to break new ground and to win fresh plaudits; 2006 was momentous for her, and 2007 promised to be just as rewarding. What better way to begin than by being selected to receive a Lifetime Achievement Award from the National Academy of Recording Arts & Sciences? Also, she was to return to the UK and Europe, following up on a recent tour she undertook that was a smash. She stood in with John Mellencamp on the single "Jim Crow" for his new CD, "Freedom Road." Her new live album "Bowery Songs," based on songs she performed at the Bowery Ballroom in New York City in November of 2004, adds fresh perspective. As a folk singer, songwriter and advocate for people from Africa to South America who are caught in the maelstrom of chaos and conflict, Joan Baez has demonstrated that most admirable of assets from the moment she broke through at the Newport Folk Festival in 1959 to the present day…staying power.

> **Wherever the road leads, however far one roams, despite the yearnings we felt as teenagers to "get away" and discover new worlds, something keeps bringing us back to the place we first knew…the place we call home.**

Once, in Endicott, New York—an old shoe town that has literally "lost its 'sole' "—there existed a pastoral setting that Russ Avery of Myrtle Beach, South Carolina remembers well.

The spot stretched all the way from Main Street on the north for several hundred yards to the Susquehanna River. People entered the grounds through "a beautiful gate" that was inscribed with the word "Casino," for "Casino Park."

Russ Avery, who is now in his seventies, recalls the park as "a gorgeous place with a stream running [throughout]," handsome wooden bridges traversing the stream in several spots and "very ornate wooden walkways (which later gave way to sidewalks). The park," he says, "was a horticulturist's dream. It contained large geranium beds, canna beds, daisy and Astor beds…all of the trees in the park were surrounded by wooden decks. There were benches and a number of fountains. The walkways went straight to the banks of the Susquehanna."

Avery's description of Casino Park is not much different than ones young people hear from their grandmothers about the scene they could expect to find upon reaching the edge of Heaven.

Before the shoe company—Endicott Johnson, or EJ—changed "much of the topography (eliminating the stream, for example) to better accommodate masses of people" and in the process destroying the aesthetic purity of the grounds, Casino Park rivaled Central Park in New York City for appeal; the sight of it startled and delighted the senses. As evidence of this, trains ran from New York City to Endicott to accommodate those who sought to spend a few hours strolling or sitting or picnicking in Casino Park.

In retrospect, its alterations in Casino Park were some of the few errors of judgment the shoe company, under the direction of its forward-thinking co-founder, George F. Johnson, made during the firm's illustrious but unfortunately short-lived history. When I came along as a youngster in the early 1950s, Casino Park had become Enjoie Park; by that time, it was known for the gargantuan pool in which kids from several neighboring communities learned to swim, a carousel that seemed to never stop turning, quiet shaded paths and a covered pavilion that provided both shelter from the storm and an opportunity to play the pinball machine.

Today, Enjoie Park is long gone. A statue of George F. Johnson marks the place where thousands from near and far found respite and rejuvenation.

Festivities associated with the 100th birthday of the village of Endicott, New York on a swelter-ing day in July of 2006 drew the owners of antique and classic automobiles to "The Avenue" for a car show. Among those present were Jerry Chambers of neighboring Johnson City who is pic-tured with his black 1949 Chevy Fleetline, affectionately dubbed "Black Ice," and Mike Lemmon of neighboring Vestal who is shown with his 1959 Ford Thunderbird. Lemmon's vehicle had approximately 70,000 miles on the odometer at the time and still sported its original paint (but no radio). Chambers and Lemmon are both originally from Endicott: "Shoe Town, USA."

Before he died in the late 1940s, George F. Johnson came close to creating as perfect a community as ever existed on American soil. Although Endicott bears the name of his partner in the formation of both the shoe company and the municipality—Henry B. Endicott—it is the legacy of George F. Johnson that locals continue to celebrate with a fervency that knows no limit. This was the case when George F. lived, with parades and company dinners and glowing tributes occurring on a regular basis in recognition of Johnson and EJ's contributions to the health and well-being of Endicott, and it is the same now even though EJ shoes, boots and sneakers for the workingman, the woman of the house and toddlers and teenagers are—like the Model T, the flintlock and the general store—a thing of the past. With observances held throughout the year in 2006 to mark Endicott's 100th anniversary, Endicotters paused once again to contemplate the significance of an arch erected in George F. Johnson's honor by EJ workers, at their own expense, in the 1920s. The arch was dedicated on Labor Day, of course! The arch, in contrast to many of the other artifacts of EJ's heyday, still stands.

Wherever they reside today, those who grew up in the Endicott of yesteryear remain fully cognizant and appreciative of the strength the village drew from EJ's benevolence; they are warmed by the thought of how lucky they were to experience it first-hand and in the undiminished sweep of its greatness—before Father Time delivered blows that proved fatal.

The European immigrants who flocked to Endicott in droves in the early 1900s to take up jobs in the factories that lined North Street, pausing only long enough to ask, in broken tongue (or occasionally in firmer command of the English language), "which way EJ?"), had heard the stories of a veritable "Oz." They yearned to see for themselves if the stories were true. As they settled in—working in multi-story wood-framed buildings constructed by EJ, frequenting shops and restaurants and movie theaters on "The Avenue" (Washington Avenue) that were a direct offshoot of the rise of EJ, purchasing "EJ houses" by payroll deduction, worshipping in churches that EJ helped midwife into being, giving birth to babies in a spectacular "hospital on the hill" that EJ saw fit to provide, playing golf on a course that EJ created for its employees (and, true to its nature, as it turned out, made available for the enjoyment of all), riding merry-go-rounds that appeared to dot every meadow —they realized that Endicott was in fact, if not the pot of gold at the end of the rainbow, at least a town worthy of their unabashed affection and allegiance.

As an industrious young man from Massachusetts who took his aspirations and dreams west with a few dollars in his pocket in search of a career in the shoe business in the late 1800s, George F. Johnson had in the back of his mind something far bigger in scope. The result was Endicott, New York—a village in which management and labor pulled together with no overriding consideration of rank or privilege, in the manner of oarsmen participating in a race for glory. Endicott—"Home of the Square Deal"—was the culmination of his vision, as surely as a man on the moon was the outgrowth of John F. Kennedy's clarion call for the United States to enter the Space Age, or advances in ending racism are a testament to the sacrifices made by Frederick Douglass, Rosa Parks, Jackie Robinson and Martin Luther King Jr.

Today, Endicotters—the sons and daughters and grandchildren of EJ workers—are scattered across the country, and beyond; they are flung far and wide. Regardless of their current address, circumstances or age, however, they still carry in their bosom warm feelings for "the Magic City." Endicott in its prime was the quintessential American small town, awash in candy stores and ice cream parlors and bakeries and playgrounds and carnivals and fireworks displays and air shows and shops on "The Avenue" and the sort of "little pink houses" that John Mellencamp has immortalized so eloquently in song.

There is no Norman Rockwell painting to prove it is true. You'll have to take my word for it.

About the Author

Rodney Lee is an award-winning career newspaperman and the author of two previously published works: a biography of the late World War II hero Rosaire J. "Ross" Rajotte of Northbridge, Massachusetts, and a memoir of his hometown of Endicott, New York—a famous shoe-manufacturing community, in its heyday. He lives in Linwood, Massachusetts with his wife, Marie.